Advance Praise for *The SHEro Mindset*

"Reading *The Shero Mindset*, I was elevated and inspired, moved to tears, and moved to action. It is a heartfelt exploration of what it takes to not only flourish in the midst of challenges, but also grow through hardship. Thank you, Lulu, for this precious gift."

—**DR. TAL BEN-SHAHAR**, co-founder Happiness Studies Academy, author of *Happier, No Matter What: Cultivating Hope, Resilience, and Purpose in Hard Times*

"In *The SHEro Mindset*, Lulu invites us to become the SHEro of our own magical journey. She offers incredible stories that are sure to inspire freedom, wisdom, joy, love, courage, creativity and faith, bolstering us when we need it most. Lulu successfully empowers us with tools gained from her many years of studying both Positive Psychology and wholebeing happiness. As someone who is on a journey to bliss, this is definitely a book I am proud to have in my life. Bravo, my SHEro, bravo!"

—**MEG NOCERO**, Author of the Butterflies & Bliss Trilogy (*Butterfly Awakens, The Magical Guide to Bliss, Sparkle & Shine*)

"*The SHEro Mindset* takes a heartful approach to the many layers of experience that shape us. Lulu's powerful and gentle narrative tells the stories of these amazing women and their journeys from pain to resilience to happiness. Love is indeed the key to happiness."

—**KAREN GUGGENHEIM**, Founder & CEO, World Happiness Summit

"What a fabulous book! Lulu inspired me to see my journey by looking through the window of her quest. Her wit, grit, gratitude and love are intense, sincere and magical. She proposes a shift in perspective from *What is wrong with us? to There is so much right with us!* Lulu's zestful stories and exploration of the SHEro Mindset are an invitation to self-reflection and game-changing shifts. If you ask yourself, *Why should I read this book?* Lulu would suggest – and I agree – you should ask instead, *Why not?*"

ANDREA SOOCH, Psychotherapist, Adjunct Professor, Actor

The SHERO MINDSET

The
SHERO
MINDSET

7 Inspirational Stories to Empower Your Life

Maria Luisa M. Carter

NAPLES, FL

Copyright © 2022 by Maria Luisa M. Carter
All rights reserved.

Published in the United States by
O'Leary Publishing
www.olearypublishing.com

Discounts available for organizations. Please email admin@olearypublishing.com for wholesale pricing.

The views, information, or opinions expressed in this book are solely those of the authors involved and do not necessarily represent those of O'Leary Publishing, LLC.

The author has made every effort possible to ensure the accuracy of the information presented in this book. However, the information herein is sold without warranty, either expressed or implied. Neither the author, publisher, nor any dealer or distributor of this book will be held liable for any damages caused either directly or indirectly by the instructions or information contained in this book. You are encouraged to seek professional advice before taking any action mentioned herein.

All rights reserved. No part of this book may be reproduced or transmitted in any form by any means, electronic, mechanical, photocopy, recording, or other without the prior and express written permission of the author, except for brief cited quotes. For information on getting permission for reprints and excerpts, contact: O'Leary Publishing.

ISBN (hardcover): 978-1-952491-99-3
ISBN (ebook): 978-1-952491-38-2
Library of Congress Control Number: 9781952491375

Editing by Heather Davis Desrocher
Proofreading by Boris Boland
Cover Design by Christine Dupre
Interior Design by Jessica Angerstein
Printed in the United States of America

To my SHEroes
My mother Linda Lislane,
my grandmother Lita and my aunt Gracinha,
Julia, Evonn, Holly, Suzy, Alexia and Didi.
To all women who are going through challenges,
remember – you too can have the SHEro Mindset!

The SHEro Mindset speaks to the pain and challenges of life, and shows the power and strength of the human spirit. These inspirational stories are examples of the transformational arc of healing. They demonstrate Positive Psychology in action. Through cultivating, choosing, and applying the science of whole being and happiness, the SHEroes have become their best possible selves – despite what life has dealt them. Each story will touch your heart and help you move from fear and isolation into self-compassion and connection with others. May we support and hold each other's hands and hearts as we heal together.

DR. NANCY KIRSNER
CERTIFIED POSITIVE PSYCHOLOGIST

Contents

Foreword i

The SHEro Mindset 1

Chapter 1 Freedom 5

    Lulu's Story – Empowered Woman
Empowers Women 7

    Seven Tips to Cultivate a SHEro Mindset 44

    Inspiration to Free Yourself 45

    Freedom Meditation 47

Chapter 2 Wisdom 49

    Julia's Story – The Nature Within 53

    Inspiration to Cultivate Wisdom 68

    Wisdom Meditation 70

Chapter 3 Joy 71

    Evonn's Story – Lessons of the Divine 75

    Inspiration to Experience Joy 97

    Joy Meditation 99

Chapter 4 Love 101

    Holly's Story – Devotion to Others 105

    Inspiration to Embody Love 126

    Love Meditation 128

Chapter 5 Courage 129
    Suzy's Story – Connections Beyond Life 133
    Inspiration to Live Courageously 156
    Courage Meditation 157

Chapter 6 Creativity 159
    Alexia's Story – The Can-Do Attitude 163
    Inspiration to Be Creative 181
    Creativity Meditation 182

Chapter 7 Faith 183
    Didi's Story – Life Is What You Make It 185
    Inspiration to Have Faith 213
    Faith Meditation 215

Conclusion 217

Reflections for a SHEro 221

The 7 Angels 227

Acknowledgments 235

About the Author 237

Foreword

This is a book unlike any book you have ever read. Why? Because the process of creating it was unique, and because the seven women who share their stories in this book have experienced what most of us can hardly imagine. Their courage to persevere, through unimaginable challenges, will touch your heart and inspire you to overcome any obstacle you face.

Writing a book is rewarding, but it can test us. Telling our story and sharing our experiences compels us to go deeply into who we are, and we are not always prepared for what we find. Writing a book that includes seven different people adds another layer of complexity. When the stories that need to be shared involve the death of children, the loss of our abilities, or life-threatening medical conditions, the task can be almost impossible – especially when the stories being told are still unfolding. It takes a SHEro Mindset to create the book you are holding in your hands.

This book project began as a way for Lulu Carter to share her passion for Positive Psychology and the journey that brought her to live a life of freedom, global connections, and joy. But as we worked on the book, it became clear that the book was about so much more than one woman's journey. This book is about the universal journey we all share as humans. It is about becoming the SHEro that our loved ones need us to be, and the SHEro that the world needs.

Each woman in this book embodies a virtue that empowered her to live her story. May you find in the pages of this book the virtues and inspiration to live your life more fully. May you have the **freedom** to realize your dreams. May you have the **wisdom** to make your knowledge useful. May you experience **joy** frequently. May **love** guide your interactions. May you draw on **courage** to move through challenges. May **creativity** allow you to express yourself authentically. May **faith** replace your fears.

HEATHER DAVIS DESROCHER
HEAD EDITOR, O'LEARY PUBLISHING

THE SHERO MINDSET

Welcome to the *SHEro Mindset!*

What is a SHEro? Is it a female hero? Yes, according to the dictionary. A SHEro is one **who thrives by choosing a resilient mindset when facing uncertainty.** Wait, there is more… the **S** adds meaning to the word, as the **S** can also stand for the word **solidarity**, from the Latin word **solidum**, which means "whole sum." Solidarity is the feeling that brings us together as part of a greater whole.

We live in a world of division, loss, anxiety and grief. We face many difficult issues: the COVID 19 pandemic, political crises, oppression, poverty, violence, racial discrimination, war and more. We definitely need more SHEroes.

We are constantly developing and learning and so role models become important to us. They motivate us to uncover our true potentials and overcome our weaknesses. I know six women who, over the years, have encouraged me to become wiser and stronger. I am incredibly grateful for these ladies: Julia, Evonn, Holly, Suzy, Alexia and Didi. I have known them for many years through our personal interaction at House of Gaia nonprofit community center. My mother and I founded House of Gaia in 2008 as a center for social inclusion in Naples, Florida. It is my happy place.

Throughout this book, seven women, including me, will each share her life's journey – illustrating the importance of values and virtues. These SHEroes recognize their difficulties, embrace their strengths, and understand how their actions and attitudes affect their lives. They have been brave to relive their past and share their stories with us. They have all experienced challenges, losses and tragedies. Yet, they have made the choice to follow the paths of love, kindness and happiness.

The Process

The process of writing this book has been profound and meaningful in my life, and it only happened as a result of my daily meditation practice. I started to meditate in the 1970s at the age of 14 with my grandfather Lesko and my mother Lis, who were studying metaphysics and energy work in Brazil. I was fascinated by learning how to quiet my thoughts and bring harmony to my life.

Meditation allowed me to overcome anxiety and fear, confront challenges, connect me with self-love, and experience internal peace. I felt my conscience expanding, and from then on, I listened to my intuition and messages from my higher conscience. To this day, I feel so empowered when I practice meditation, both alone or with a group.

My spirituality gave me the courage to cross many oceans, lands and continents to find the connections to fulfill my purpose. God was answering my prayers to meet incredible people who helped to shape my life.

Over the years, I also developed a very strong connection with angels. These beings continue to play a major role in my life, guiding me to stay focused on the positive things. The angels help me to gather the courage to confront my fears, and also motivate me to spread love and joy as I move through life.

Yet, over all those years, I could never find the time to write this book. It was only during the lockdown in 2020 that the first pages of this book started to come alive. It was time to explore the bravery of the women I know and the incredible stories of their resilience. We were all in need of more bravery in 2020.

This book crystallized into a platform for presenting seven inspirational stories. I was able to spend wonderful quality time with Julia, Evonn, Holly, Suzy, Alexia and Didi – talking, sharing, crying and laughing. What we experienced was intense, sincere and magical. Listening to them and processing their stories was a gift, and revisiting my past was healing. This process was genuine and sacred.

During that magical time, I became stronger. We were all going through something; all of us were challenged by the pandemic. We were writing about the past and we had to be SHEroes to give birth to this book.

The Mandalas

During the process of writing, I meditated to gain clarity and to empower myself to deliver these messages. During a group meditation session at House of Gaia, I was inspired to create a mandala for each chapter. Each mandala was inspired by one of the angel affirmation cards I had created; the angel cards were life-changing for me. The geometric configurations of the symbols represent our spiritual journey. Mandalas are used in Hinduism and Buddhism; one moves toward the center in the process of transforming suffering into joy.

The mandalas also represent the journey of each SHEro. Each story in this book – like the mandalas – starts from the outside and moves to the inner core, through layers. May the stories of each SHEro inspire you to expand and heal your heart, mind and soul. May they lead you toward a more fulfilling, peaceful and happy life.

The Power of
FREEDOM

Freedom is authentic self-expression in words, movement, and actions without inhibition. It gives us permission to feel and make choices. The power of Freedom exists when responsibility, fairness and justice become the result of everyone's action to benefit the sum, not only one individual. Freedom cannot exist without moral choices.

*Art can be the guardian of its freedom.
It resists authoritarianism by encouraging
critical discourse and creative autonomy.
In fact, I believe that arts' practice
is the practice of freedom!*

REGINA MIRANDA

CHAPTER 1
Freedom

Lulu's Story
Empowered Woman Empowers Women

Freedom has always been the dominant theme in my life. I had to be brave and creative to move beyond my own limitations and society's barriers. From a young age, I was blessed to understand how important it is to use my strengths and virtues while on my journey. My resilience, gratitude, and love of learning have helped me create a full and happy life. My father gave me wings to fly; the encouragement to do whatever I wanted in life.

My mother raised me to be independent. But I could not have survived my darkest moments if I had not felt solidarity with others – that spiritual sense of belonging to an energetic and cosmic family of people who share my values, mission and purpose. In fact, it was my spirituality that helped me to find freedom even if I became trapped. Because even if you are fleeing from a war or experiencing a hard situation, your spirit can still be free.

The Miracle

My story is one of challenges, which drove me to find freedom. For me, even being conceived was a challenge. In 1963, my parents lived in Brazil and had been struggling to have a baby. My mother Lislane was 20 years old, and my father Malta was 26 years old. My parents' persistence led them to find the right doctor. After two years and many trials, my mother finally became pregnant with me! Can you imagine the likelihood of being conceived in a Brazilian doctor's office back in 1965? Indeed, I was a miracle! And I never took my life for granted.

My First SHEroes

From an early age, I was introduced to a gratitude practice by my SHEroes. These women shaped my mindset, taught me valuable lessons, and helped me understand the depth of a life lived with virtues.

My first childhood SHEro was my mom Lislane, or Lis for short. She was stunning, intelligent, and ahead of her time. She was a Renaissance woman with a master's degree in psychology, living and adventuring in the Brazilian Amazon. My mom had a passion for philanthropy and was always ready to help someone in need.

My second childhood SHEro was my grandmother Lita. She was a unique person – funny, eccentric, strong in character; and she had a heart of gold. She was a dedicated wife who raised six children, and many grandchildren and great-grandchildren. Grandma Lita volunteered at local orphanages in Brazil and was an excellent church singer.

My third childhood SHEro was my aunt Gracinha, who is very kind, fun and wise. We share common interests and similar struggles – like anxiety – and I can talk to her very openly. Like my mother and grandmother, she is an amazing wife, mother and grandmother, and family is important to her like it is to me. I am so blessed to still have her in my life.

A Country of Contrasts

I am Brazilian, and Brazil is a land of contrasts, where one can experience the full spectrum of life. It is one of the most beautiful countries I have known; yet, its history is full of exploitation and slavery. Brazil is rich, and it is poor. Brazilians are free, and yet they have been oppressed.

As a child, my life included vast contrasts. I attended a conservative Catholic school and went to church on Sundays, where I learned about Jesus and core values. But then I watched as the oppressive military government controlled the lives of Brazilians. I could not grasp the mismatch between the values taught in my school and the misbehavior of my peers, the politicians, and Brazilian society. Even though I was so young, I was very aware of everything around me.

In that environment, one could go from feeling happy to feeling stressed out in the space of just a few seconds. So, growing up in Brazil was fun, yet difficult.

I was an imaginative child. I was creative and an outside-the-box thinker, and because of that, my friends thought I was weird. I did not fit in and felt no sense of community with my peers. That led to severe anxiety for much of my childhood. I prayed to God to set me free from my anxiety, but my prayers were not answered at that moment.

I remember my first panic attack, at the age of 6. It was late at night. I could not sleep, and I was afraid. It felt like I had stopped breathing. I wanted to stick my head inside of a refrigerator to breathe some cold air into my lungs.

I mentioned that my aunt Gracinha also had experiences with anxiety. I loved going to her house, talking with her, and not having to hide my feelings. With her, I felt seen and heard; this was in a time when no one talked about mental health issues. My cousin Paola (the daughter of my uncle Lesko) was also very important to my development. Just a year younger than I, Paola was my best friend and a sister to me. We were inseparable. When I was with her, I felt understood – she joined me in my world of imagination.

At the age of 9, my life changed completely when my father decided to move us from São Paulo to Rio de Janeiro. Because of the move, Mom and I were separated from her family. Rio de Janeiro was foreign to us and I felt alone; it took a few years for me to learn the culture and make new friends. I attended a wonderful Catholic school, Colégio Marista São José, in the neighborhood of Tijuca.

Losing My Innocence

When I was 11, my mother and I were visiting her family in São Paulo during Easter when her body rejected the fertility treatment she was given. She was having a lot of pain in her belly and she began hemorrhaging. She had to have a hysterectomy, and lost so much blood that we were not sure she would survive.

I did not ask any questions about my mother's condition. Instead, I immersed myself in the world of my imagination. My coping mechanism during that time was art: drawing and coloring. My mother almost lost her life, and she forever lost her dream of having another child. I prayed for a miracle; I could not imagine life without my SHEro.

And that time my prayers were answered. I got the news that my mother would survive and return home. Gratitude grew in my heart, as I learned that life could change in the blink of an eye.

The innocence of my childhood was swept away by traumatic experiences.

I suffered sexual abuse by a family member. As a teenager, even though my body was fully developed, I still had the mind of a child. I was embarrassed to admit it, but at the age of 14, I still played with my Barbies.

My life course changed when someone who I admired and trusted started to develop a sexual interest in me. I felt ashamed and dirty. I wondered why it was happening, and I questioned the values I had learned in Catholic school and at home. The experience caused me terrible emotional pain and trauma.

So, I was triggered with negative feelings, all over again, since I had also been molested when I was 3 years old. That was likely another reason that I suffered anxiety and panic attacks as a child. Wouldn't you think so?

Why wasn't I rescued by my SHEroes or by my guardian angel? My youth was simply stolen from me, and my innocence was lost forever. I carried a secret inside of me – how awful. I had to learn how to hide my feelings and my shame. No one should have gone through that experience. No one.

It took me a lifetime of therapy to recognize the emotional scars left from the abuse. I often wonder what my life would have been like if I had not suffered that abuse.

One Door Closes and Another Opens

My life reflected the contrasts of my country, Brazil. I had many blessings too, and one of the blessings of my childhood was dance. I started to dance when I was 7. I have vivid memories of my dance school, and of how happy I was dancing with my friends as a fairy. Dancing helped me to come out of my shell.

By the age of 16, I was being trained as a professional modern dance teacher at a prestigious dance studio in Rio de Janeiro, which was led by Enid Sauer. "Tia Enid" had two daughters, Elena and Cristina, who were wonderful. They were associated with the Joffrey Ballet from New York, and my love for American culture started in their dance school. I even traveled with friends to the United States on my first trip abroad.

Unfortunately, I had an accident during the filming of a jazz class for television, and I tore all the ligaments in my left knee. After emergency surgery, it took a year of physical therapy just to learn how to walk again. Sadly, I had to quit professional dance, but I longed to go back to dance in some way someday.

As one door closed, another was opening. I was destined to meet my first two mentors: Regina Miranda (a teacher of the Laban Method) and Angel Vianna (a teacher of contemporary-style dance), the two most amazing dance teachers in Brazil. They encouraged me to learn new ways to move my body. And instead of only learning dance, I was learning the most important lessons of my life: how to love myself and the power of body expression. After many hours of incredible exercises, I started to release the fears of expressing myself, hurting my body, and connecting deeply with others.

A Downward Spiral

Over the years, partly because of the sexual abuse, I developed severe anxiety and an eating disorder. By the time I was 18, there were other family problems in my life, and I felt so lost. I had no confidence that my SHEroes would be able to stand by me. In fact, all of them were battling their own challenges.

My mother was suicidal – she was in despair over her life and her marriage – and she decided to leave our house to find her own identity and simply survive. I was left to live with my father and my granny Lita. My grandfather Lesko died of cancer at age 64, and granny, at 63, was very depressed. My father started to lose his mind over cocaine, which played a large part in high society in Brazil in the 1980s. My father was rich; and with Rio de Janeiro being a violent place, I received kidnapping threats.

Going to college was challenging, and over time I developed social anxiety. I had trouble focusing and it was hard to complete simple tasks. Thankfully, my mentors Regina Miranda and Angel Viana helped me to feel somewhat grounded during dance classes. They did not know that their kindness and interest in helping me to overcome my fears meant the world to me.

My first boyfriend, Lincoln, and I attended the same art college. His parents were divorcing as well, and we were too young to cope with everything. After four years in our codependent relationship, he decided to end it. My heart was broken, and I felt I could never love again. I was forced to learn how to be alone.

Changing Direction

At 21, I was ready for a change – I was ready for freedom from my country and from my parents, and from all the worries they had given me. One evening, I was walking on campus and saw a poster advertising an English course in Ramsgate, England. The poster called my name! I stopped and took a deep breath. I was fascinated by the picture of the world map. There was an arrow pointing from Brazil to the other side of the Atlantic Ocean – to England!

Immediately, my soul was transported. I had visited Europe a few years before and I could see myself there in a heartbeat! I was filled with positive emotions and a renewed desire for living.

I had been saving money from the time I was 14 and working as a ballet teacher. I also sold clothes and decorated children's birthday parties. I was saving the money for my wedding with Lincoln. It sounds funny now... married at the age of 21? What a silly thought! Since there would be no wedding, I felt I could use the money for a better cause – to claim my freedom from the roles that had been given to me.

I called a family meeting – I had never done that before – and advised my parents that I was moving to England to spend a gap year learning English... and to learn about myself. Both of my parents were really surprised! My mom did not take the news well at all. She wanted me to finish college in Rio. Those times were different – people did not just put their lives on hold to travel or live in another country. With no internet at that time, the world was very big and mysterious.

But my parents' opinions did not matter to me, anyway. I was 100 percent committed to this new life of adventure and I felt entitled to my happiness. I said YES! I was free to choose my own destiny and ready to become my best self. So, my courage and desire to learn took me halfway around the world.

Flying High

I arrived in England and had my first shock. I was coming from a tropical sunny country with an exotic culture. Ramsgate, on the other hand, was snowy, damp and gloomy. Nevertheless, the weather would not stop me in my journey of self-discovery.

The day after my arrival, I woke up early to a white sky, cold air, and thick fog. I could not find my way to school, as everything looked the same with the snow piled high. I kept feeling that I was lost, but I managed to arrive at the Churchill House School by foot. I was so excited! I was a fish out of water, but I was eager to learn about everything around me.

I found a chair close to the teacher, but soon I felt my social anxiety acting up. My breath became short, and I was about to have a meltdown. Then I decided to stop the negative thoughts. I looked around me and let the beauty of the diversity of my fellow students be my focus – there were so many people with different accents, skin colors, haircuts, and fashions. I was so incredibly grateful – and at the same time, very curious about them.

My tiny English-language school was a melting pot, and it made me feel like I had found my home – a safe home. The first friend I made in England was Paula, another girl from Brazil. Although she was only 15 years old, she was wise and mature. I still had the mindset of a dancer, and I was borderline anorexic. Paula would check on me to make sure I was eating. She helped me a great deal with my anxiety and my eating disorder. I felt accepted by her and was happy to be included in her life.

Soon, I was letting go of my fears, little by little, even though it was my first time living in another country. It was a bit intimidating. However, I had the freedom to make choices; those opportunities were priceless. I came out of my shell and became more extroverted.

During the school semester, I had many adventures with my new friends. They were so nice to me, and we had so much fun. Raquel and I traveled to Scotland, Belgium, Paris, and Holland; we experienced the freedom of traveling around Europe on trains. I had the freedom to say "no" to the drugs in Amsterdam (I was afraid of losing my mind like my father had, so I never tried drugs) and to say "yes" to chocolate in Belgium (I was learning how to savor a nice chocolate without the fear of putting on weight).

The Price of Freedom

One night I met an Englishman, who was 23, at a pub. After spending some time dancing with him, he invited me to see his house. I was feeling confident, and I was excited that this most handsome man had noticed me among so many other beautiful girls. I was sober and just looking for a date and a couple of kisses.

I remember arriving at his place and sitting on the sofa. That was my last real memory that night.

I felt that my body had gone to war, and I felt as if there were 100 soldiers running over me. It was only one man, for a couple of hours, spinning my body everywhere, until he was finished... finally satisfied. I immediately ran to the bathroom afterward. I looked at myself in the mirror and I couldn't see my face. Everything was foggy and I noticed that my hair was completely messed up. My soul had left my body; I felt totally disassociated from my true self.

I was afraid to return to the other room and see him again. I didn't want to have to look at his eyes. But I had to leave that house immediately. So, I told him I had to go home – because if my roommate Paula didn't see me on my bed, she would call the police and report me missing. I grabbed my bag, and I don't even know how I found a taxi. It was early in the morning.

I told the driver to take me to the nearest hospital. The doctor that saw me noticed black and purple marks all over my legs, back, neck and belly. I felt so sore. He wanted me to report the case. I was so afraid of exposing myself, being a foreign student. I just wanted to go home and forget everything. I was deeply wounded – spiritually, physically and emotionally. Silence became my friend.

I shared my experience with no one, not even my mother or my best friends. I was the only witness of my rape. I was in shock, and I went into complete denial.

I had learned that freedom came with responsibilities. I knew I had to be responsible for my feelings and my actions. But I was not the one who caused my rape. I was the victim. I was looking for romance, not violent sex. The experience taught me that I had to learn how to forgive myself first, and then forgive him. I now hold everyone accountable, including myself. To heal, I also needed to learn to forgive everyone who had crossed my path.

Cultivating Positive Memories

After four months in England, I decided to extend my European trip to Italy. I needed to explore other places and build new memories.

But before I left for Italy, my mother came to inspect my life, like a good Brazilian mom. My father had already been to visit me at the beginning of my trip. I liked being with my mother, but she made me nervous. She had the power to see into my soul and perhaps find my secrets.

Nevertheless, I needed her approval because my funds were running out. I needed her to sponsor the rest of my time in Europe. I trusted my parents enough to ask for their help.

Mom arrived and we had a great reunion. Everyone thought we were sisters because she was so young and beautiful. My best friend Paula joined us, and we toured Europe again (it's the best playground for adults). We wanted to explore, to see other cultures, and to try other foods. I was anxious to speak what little German I knew.

We visited friends in Germany, Austria and Switzerland. I danced a waltz with my mom in Vienna; and we toured Paris, visiting Galeries Lafayette, the Louvre, and Montmartre. I shared a beer with my mom; I can still close my eyes and taste that cold beer all these years later. The funny thing is, we are not drinkers... we were just being silly together. We had created golden memories by the time Mom's visit ended in Paris – memories that I still treasure today. France and its culture became a big part of my life: Mom's favorite song was "La Vie En Rose," and my favorite book became *Le Petit Prince*.

So, she returned to Brazil with the knowledge that I could be independent and healthy – and most importantly, connected to people with the same values and goals. She decided to sponsor the rest of my trip in Europe.

She was proud of what I had become. I was creating my own story, with my own patterns. I was learning that I could still be me, even though I was being helped. Being humble is part of feeling free!

The Awakening

After my mom left for Brazil, I was ready for the next chapter of life: studying art and Italian during the summer. And so I left on a new adventure.

When I arrived in the medieval town of Siena at 5 a.m., everything was closed. *Where should I go?* I immediately thought, and I answered my own question: *Let me go to a church; the doors will be open, and I will be safe there!*

I found my way to the Chiostro San Domenico, one of the most majestic and unique churches in Siena. I had arrived in heaven at this empty, peaceful church. I will never forget Chiostro San Domenico – it is set on top of a small hill, surrounded by pine trees, with an incredible view of the Duomo.

I laid down on one of the benches to rest after the long trip. I felt peace – God was in my heart and had granted me serenity. I was introspective, not knowing what the future held. I was alone, but I was not lonely. It felt like a dream. I fell asleep....

I woke up to the sound of the tower bells ringing and Italians speaking loudly as they arrived for morning Mass. Every single sound helped to awaken my soul. After what had happened to me on the night of my rape in England, I needed to be rescued from my own shame. I felt a shift in my core. My body was being cleansed; my spirit was being lifted from feelings of not being worthy. And it was like a blessing – I woke up with a brand-new attitude and the desire to experience life anew.

I was energized and ready to start my art studies. I moved into my new place with my Canadian roommates. Our apartment was outside the medieval walls, and the ceilings were painted with frescos. My roommates were so inclusive and helpful, and I loved them. We went for long walks to school, up and down the hills of Siena. Life was so exciting.

Siena is a truly beautiful medieval city, surrounded by a long brick wall with gates. The architecture is breathtaking – there are many statues of angels, and in every corner, there are more statues, fountains, and history.

I found freedom in learning new things, in immersing myself in the arts, and in making friends from all over the world. Watching the Italians speak helped me to liberate myself and to become more extroverted and talkative. I was proud of myself.

My friends and I bravely hitchhiked from Siena to Florence; it was OK, since everyone did it. That was the norm. I was going to museums, drawing, sketching, and observing the rhythm of life in Italy. One of my Canadian roommates, Rita, and I took a couple of weeks off to visit Florence. Rita showed me kindness and led me to experience life with confidence, as I expanded my knowledge and conscience.

The food in Italy was superb, and I let go of my fear of putting on weight. For the first time, I savored pasta and sweets. It was like I was tasting the first food in my life. I went crazy with Italian pop songs, concerts, and fashion. I was alive!

I loved hopping on the train to travel. It was just me, my red backpack, and a stuffed teddy bear who traveled with me as an emotional support pillow. Every time I missed someone, I hugged my teddy bear pillow.

The Wall and the War

I was ready to explore as much as I could. Eventually, I went to visit Dorothy, a friend I met in Siena. She lived in Berlin. She and I got along very well, and she wanted me to spend time with her family. I did not hesitate to accept her invitation, and said YES. As I crossed from West to East Berlin by train, I felt myself transported to a tragic era in history. I was mesmerized by the remains of the infamous Berlin Wall. *How did such a thing happen?* It created a scar among German families and friends as they were separated. Just the thought of the Wall made me a little bit anxious.

Dorothy's father was so nice and helped me put things in perspective. He was very generous with his time and wanted to explain the traumas Germany had both caused and suffered through, from World War II into the Cold War. I was shocked when he showed me all the bullet marks on his home's walls from the Allied invasion of Berlin in 1945.

Then he took me to Auschwitz camp. I could feel his shame as I saw the hundreds of shoes and boots of the Jews killed in the concentration camp. I saw their hair and their shoes on the floor, which were removed upon their arrival. I wondered how humanity could be so cruel.

Even though the Holocaust was one of the worst times that humanity has experienced, there were also stories of brave individuals facing uncertainties. Mothers and fathers developed their own hero mindsets as they took measures to save their children. I was in awe of their determination to survive. I also heard stories about solidarity; how people with different religions and backgrounds shared the same values. They put their lives at risk to help the Jews.

Those stories warmed my heart and gave me hope for humanity's future. Going to Berlin was an eye-opening experience at the age of 21 – a moment in my life that I will never forget.

Haunted by My Past

After my year in Europe, I felt empowered, renewed, and proud that I had accomplished my goals. I wanted to return to my own country, as I truly missed my Brazilian culture, family, and friends. I was ready to live in Rio and restart college. Traveling abroad had expanded my mind. By being away from my family, I became more aware of the many roles that had been given to me since I was born. But I wanted to shed some roles and create new ones as well. My mindset had changed from fragile to fearless, and I returned to Brazil as more my authentic self. However, as much as I wanted to take on a role as a free young woman, I still did not feel confident enough to be completely free, given the scary and chaotic reality at home in Brazil.

Things with my family were not good at all. My father was a force of life; very adventurous, very charismatic. Unfortunately, because of stress and social pressures, he had started to use drugs.

And because he was distracted by mounting a political campaign, he was losing his multimillion-dollar business. My beautiful mother was trying to save our family from bankruptcy while also taking care of her mother, who was suffering from depression. She was also looking after her younger brother, who was dying of AIDS at only 38 years old.

My uncle Delano was the best uncle ever. At that time, there was no treatment for the HIV virus. Seeing him lose his hair, his weight, his skin, his teeth, his mind... was awful. But the worst thing was the sound of silence in my family. No one talked about the fact that he was gay. That topic is still taboo in my mother's family.

The loss of my uncle meant the loss of joy in Mom's family. My grandmother Lita was devastated and lost the sparkle in her eyes, and the beat of her heart. My mother and aunt Gracinha lost their best friend. After his death, everything changed.

My uncle gave me the gift of witnessing a person's transformation. And just like the journey that a butterfly takes, I watched him go through his own journey to release his spirit from its vessel... from the prison of his body to the freedom of his soul. It was extremely sad, yet very powerful.

The Rising Phoenix

At the age of 23, my horizon suddenly became smaller. Losing my uncle made me shut down. As a reaction, I impulsively decided to marry one of my friends, Tarso. My best friends, Paula and Alexandra, advised me not to marry him; they could see what we couldn't. Tarso was young, and I was so desperate to escape my own reality.

We had first met as teens on summer holidays in Arraial do Cabo, a popular beach destination in Rio de Janeiro. He was young and idealistic and had become my best friend. I thought I could escape my reality by marrying him and building my own family with my core values.

I always wanted to become a mother, but I did not expect to become pregnant right after my wedding. But I would not question it; how could I? After all, my parents struggled to have me. And look! I got pregnant so easily. I felt so grateful; so blessed.

During the beginning of my pregnancy, I was exuberant and confident. However, after my fifth month of pregnancy, Tarso started to change. He did not want to engage with my body or my belly.

I had never experienced a rejection like that before. The emotional pain was hard to bear; my self-esteem plummeted. I thought pregnancy was going to be the happiest time of my life, but it ended up being confusing, hurtful and unpredictable. My anxiety level went through the roof; I developed high blood pressure, which put my life and the baby's life at risk. When it was time for the delivery, I was rushed to the hospital for an emergency C-section. Thankfully, with good doctors and with God, we were fine, and my baby was healthy.

I named my boy Mateus, which means "the gift from God." He truly was a gift, born to change my life forever. Because of Mateus, I had to discover my powers and grow stronger.

Tarso did not know how to handle the pressure of becoming a father. Out of fear, he chose to stop following his dream, and instead became part of the system to pay the bills. He was unhappy; he started to drink more and smoked marijuana with his friends. He had affairs and did not engage emotionally with Mateus or me. I felt abandoned and hurt, and became very lonely. My marriage was dying, and I was left alone emotionally to raise my son.

I was saved by the people in my support system, who helped me to raise my son with the integrity and dignity that we deserved. My aunt Gracinha always invited me to go to her house in Santos, São Paulo. There, I loved to take a nice walk at the shore, play with my young cousins, and order Chinese food. Mateus and I were always welcomed, and it felt safe in her house. I could be me, even with all my anxiety. Simple living brought joy to my life.

I also felt so grateful for my parents' and friends' unconditional love. Paula and Alexandra were always checking on me – drying my tears, rescuing me from panic attacks. Other people's acts of kindness helped me along the way.

But even with all of the support, I was barely functioning. My self-esteem was very low and I was becoming codependent again. Even though I tried everything to save my marriage, Tarso's behavior was becoming more and more erratic. He would say, "I love you" and "I hate you" at nearly the same time, and those mixed messages drove me crazy. When we fought about it, he became violent. One time, Tarso kicked me, almost breaking my leg. Another time, he hit my face while I was holding Mateus in my arms. He even threatened to kill me. Was he joking? I did not know for sure, and I was consumed by fear. I had become a prisoner of my marriage and lived in constant dread.

One afternoon, my mother stopped by my house to check on me. She said, "Filha (daughter), who are you? I look into your eyes, and I don't see you anymore." My soul felt crushed. My parents and my friends did not recognize me anymore. And I could not go on anymore with that life of abuse.

Deep down, I knew that something had to change. I needed to free myself yet again. This time, I needed to be free from a dysfunctional and oppressive relationship. I remembered the story of the phoenix, and felt that I too could go through the fire to find myself reborn again. My spirituality gave me the courage to make a change and free myself.

Becoming a SHEro!

I knew I had to do better for both Mateus and myself. *Can I stay and grow stronger in my relationship with Tarso, or do I have the courage to simply leave him?* After thinking a lot about it, I found that I had enough courage to pack my bags and take my 3-year-old boy with me. I was done with Tarso. After he betrayed me with a married woman in my own house, I did not have any hope for our relationship. I also no longer had any respect for him. I wanted the freedom to choose my life; to be creative again, to think on my own, and to have my own voice – as I once had before.

The worst parts of my marriage were feeling rejected and seeing my child neglected by his father. The best part of my marriage was the birth of Mateus. My son was the best thing that had happened in my life, and I wanted him to grow up with a happier mother. I wanted Mateus to be free to make his own choices and live his own dreams.

For my son, I had to become a SHEro.

Becoming a SHEro was not easy... and, as much as I was ready to spread my wings and be free to live my best life, incorporating the SHEro mindset was really challenging. I was alone as a single mom at 29, and I faced a litigious divorce battle to win custody of Mateus and have the freedom to raise him without emotional abuse. I had to find the strength to win full custody of my son.

The SHEro's Struggle

As I was going through the custody battle, my father was diagnosed with hepatitis C and his organs started to fail. There was no treatment for hepatitis C in the early '90s. But because of his love for Mateus – his only grandson – he became sober and helped me raise my baby boy. He became the best grandfather in the world. I was so proud of my dad.

At the same time, my mother and I gathered the courage to open a bilingual preschool and child care center in Rio. We wanted to create a safe space for Mateus to grow with friends and family, surrounded by love.

My family supported me; my grandmother Lita took great care of me and her great-grandson. My uncle Douglas – my mother's youngest brother – invited Mateus and me to travel with him and his daughter Izaura (along with another cousin, Denise) to get away from my troubles. Each of these kind people who passed through my life brought me a little hope during a terrible time.

At the same time, I recognized my limits, and I asked for help from loved ones, mental health professionals, healers, friends and even strangers. I was so thankful for my SHEroes and for everyone who played a role in my life to keep my baby and me safe.

I surrendered my will and spirituality to a power greater than myself. I asked my angels to guide me through the darkness; they helped me to become my best self. Archangel Michael, with his sword, was there to clear my path. My angels were very important – they were there to protect me, to provide answers, to give me courage, and to rebuild my confidence.

Slowly and surely, I started to heal. My healing came out of meditation – from the practice of staying still, cleaning my mind of negative thoughts, and feeling gratitude.

I was gently rebirthing myself. I went for long bike rides, started to dance again, and experienced the freedom of travel again. I started to reconnect with friends and rekindled the feelings of hope and confidence.

Those were difficult times. Because of Tarso's determination to ruin my life, I could have lost custody of my son – or even my life. I was so young, but I was determined to advocate for my son's best interests – as a human and as a mother – despite my fears.

Saying Yes to Happiness
And just like that… when I least expected it, happiness knocked on my door! Sometimes we can be surprised by a good thing! At that point in my life, I was completely closed to a relationship and did not want anything to do with love. And yet, I was about to open my heart again.

Even though I had zero desire to socialize, my best friend Paula (from my time in England) and my mother insisted that I go to a dinner with friends. Despite my lack of interest in meeting anyone, Paula introduced me to a man during dinner. Adam was originally from New York and had a travel company in Rio. I found him to be sincere, charismatic, and handsome. That night, on September 18, 1994, our lives were changed forever.

Our first meeting transformed into a date that was romantic and real! That night, I knew that I had met my soulmate, because when I looked into his blue eyes I could see his soul. What a beautiful person, I thought. I felt safe and protected, yet emotional.

On our second date, we spent a lot of time getting to know each other on a very deep level. We shared our fears, our losses, and our dreams. We did not hide anything from each other.

Our chemistry was off the charts, and I was shocked when Adam asked me to marry him after our third date. And to everyone's surprise, I said YES! I know it was impulsive, but Adam and I were compelled by forces we could not see. Our need to live life as a couple was powerful and it allowed me to overcome my fear of a relationship.

I confess that I was needy and lost. I was ready for another codependent relationship. However, this time was different. I felt that Adam and I had to be together and start a life. Our meeting was not casual. We were part of one another. And even though we both were not yet divorced, I felt that I was emotionally free to choose him as a life partner.

Have you ever experienced something that is so powerful that you had to jump in and just say yes?

The SHEro Survives

Adam and I were engaged for two years. We did not know where we were going to spend our lives together; there was so much to figure out. Tarso did not want me to move to the United States with Adam and Mateus, and he created a series of legal barriers to prevent that from happening.

One fateful day, I was working at my preschool in Rio de Janeiro when my lawyer called. (He was my fifth lawyer, the best lawyer in Brazil, and he understood international laws.) He explained that Tarso was working on a federal level to create a document that would forever prohibit me from leaving Brazil with my son. My lawyer explained that if I ever wanted to leave my country with my son, I needed to pack my bags and depart that night. There would be no phone calls to anyone, no goodbyes. My heart stopped. I had to make the most difficult decision of my life. I had to leave my country in secret.

It was so hard to tell my parents and my granny that I was leaving, and that I did not know when we would see each other again. I was taking my son from their lives, which was ripping their hearts apart. I felt guilty, but it was the only way to do what was best for Mateus.

I call that day the day of my "death." It was one of the darkest moments of my life. I left everything behind to start all over again; I left Brazil to save my child and spare him from his father's emotional abuse.

I will never forget that evening, leaving with one bag and with my 5-year-old son holding my hand. I knew that my parents' hearts were broken. Mateus and I would be traveling to New York with Adam, who would have the responsibility of taking care of us in the United States.

I escaped the prison that Tarso had created. Sadly I was leaving behind my professional life, my family, and my friends. I cried during the entire nine-hour flight. What gave me hope was knowing that my son would finally be free.

Tarso did not believe in me, in my dreams, or in my power. He patronized me; he diminished me. However, I was happy to prove him wrong. I learned that there is nothing I cannot do if I set my mind to it, work hard, and pursue happiness.

For weeks, Tarso did not know where we were. My parents told him that I was at my aunt's house in Santos, São Paulo. Once he learned that I was not even in Brazil, he filed a case against me for kidnapping our son. Thankfully, I had left Brazil legally with an old passport for Mateus, authorizing him to travel abroad. Emotionally, however, I felt bad that I had taken my son from his country, culture, and family.

My Spirituality

I would have to rebuild my life in the United States from scratch. I was broken and fragile. Yet, I felt free. We moved to Connecticut, a one and a half hour train ride from New York, in New England. To me it seemed so cold, sad and charmless.

I did everything I had to do to survive an international divorce. I had to prove the value of my motherhood and give birth to my son for a second time. I had no idea that it would take me six years of fighting in the American and Brazilian courts to gain full custody of Mateus. It took endless hours to make a case that he should stay with me, and not with Tarso.

I was suffering from asthma, pain in my body, digestive problems, and sinus issues. I was in bad shape. I was overeating, overworking and not sleeping well. I felt raw, but never disempowered; I was devoted to our family's success. I started working with my husband in his travel business and I finished a master's degree in education.

I had my faith, which sustained me through all of my challenges. And with faith, we decided to move to Naples, Florida when Mateus was 7 years old, since I couldn't stand the cold. Naples reminded me of the Brazilian landscape with the palm trees and white sand beaches. The warm weather made me feel at home, too.

One evening, I was feeling hopeless, stressed and deeply sad. I picked up some crayons and markers and started drawing on white paper. I did not think about anything; I let my imagination flow. For me, God is creation – I am one with the universe when I am creating.

I drew an angel, and as I looked at the angel, I knew that it represented Freedom. I felt the weight of my challenges lift a bit, and so I drew another angel. I knew that this second one represented Wisdom. I kept drawing; and, in the end, I had seven beautiful angels – one for each day of the week (see pg. 227).

Each angel represented a virtue that has guided my life – Freedom, Wisdom, Joy, Love, Courage, Creativity and Faith – and each one carried an affirmational message for me. I decided to meditate every day with the angel cards and the virtues they represented. Depending on the card that I would intuitively pick, I would focus all my attention and awareness on the virtue of that card. I would let it guide my actions and attitude. For example, if I picked Joy, my day would be nothing but joyful.

The angel cards always helped me to sort out my thoughts and shift to a more positive mindset. They came to me as a present from heaven to bring peace to my heart, clarity to my mind, and light to my spirit.

Drawing those seven angels was a pivotal moment in my life. My life changed from darkness to shining light! Because of the angel cards, I started practicing mindfulness and positive thinking everyday. This practice helped me to curate my life and gain full awareness of my virtues.

Beyond the Sea

The moment I was granted the freedom to raise my son, the joy returned to my heart.

Every effort and sacrifice that I had made was worth it. Mateus and I were ready to live our lives in peace. And we could travel – not just between the United States and Brazil, but beyond those borders.

I was able to raise my son with dignity and love. As he got older, he explored the beauty of the Amazon, which influenced his career choice as an outdoor educator. He enjoyed his culture, family and friends.

We circumnavigated the globe in 2001 with Semester at Sea, an international study-abroad program. He was experiencing other cultures and different ways of living – I was giving him the world. He also had the opportunity to live in the Galapagos and be immersed in nature there.

My positive attitude and actions have kept my marriage healthy and protected me from traumas and fears. Adam and I have created a beautiful and loving family together. We raised Mateus with love and care, and I supported Adam in his relationships with his children, Michael and Julia, and with his grandchildren.

I helped Adam grow our travel business and we overcame many differences: age, culture, family patterns and communication. Our chemistry and spirituality has kept us deeply connected. Most important, Adam helps me contain my emotions by bringing me back from relapses and traumas to a safe and loving place.

Romance and Commitment

Adam and I have created and celebrated six weddings so far, each one in a different culture. Our first marriage was a symbolic ceremony in Connecticut with our mothers in attendance (our divorces were not yet final). The second, in Florida with our fathers present, was our official wedding. The third, in Las Vegas at the Chapel of Love, was just for fun. The fourth was on a ship during our trip around the world, and the captain married us. Our fifth, in Greece with just the two of us, was the best! Finally, in 2019 we were married in a Shiva temple in India to celebrate our spiritual connection. How romantic is that?

Why have we married so many times? The answer is, why not?! We wanted to celebrate our spiritual journey more than once. The multiple weddings sustain our romance and feed our passion. It is hard to describe our love for each other. We sometimes ask, "What is wrong with us?" But really, there is nothing wrong and so much right with us.

The SHEro of SHEroes

My resilience empowers me to make changes and live a full life. My divorce made me stronger, not weaker. Tarso became one of my toughest teachers; I forgave him, and through that lesson, I learned how to validate my own feelings.

I became a global citizen who traveled the world. I became the Queen Mother (a title of endearment) of Torgome, a village in Africa, and had the opportunity to travel to Haiti, helping many orphanages. Recently, I was invited to go to Romania with therapist Mary Bellofatto and a team of psychologists to help refugee children from Ukraine work through their trauma. I was honored to be invited but I decided not to go, nevertheless I want to mention this opportunity to serve in Ukraine during a war. I understand that my spirit leads me to visit places I never imagined.

Saying YES to the pursuit of happiness has changed my life. Saying YES to life has enabled me to connect with the most incredible people on this planet!

Some of my most memorable moments of service came while traveling to Haiti during times of cholera and hurricanes. I loved spending my time and sharing my purpose at the New Life Children's Home – a little heaven in the middle of the chaos of Port-au-Prince. I am truly happy when I can help others be happy – when I can help them to find their own hero mindset and live a life of peace, prosperity and love.

The SHEro Mindset

On one of our trips to Haiti, my mom met the New Life orphanage's founder, Miriam Frederick. Mom was impressed by Miriam's tenacity and her capacity to save so many children's lives. Mom told me that Miriam was the most impressive human she ever met and that she had a heart of gold. She is the SHEro of SHEroes; she has inspired me and so many others. Her mindset is limitless. She is moved by her faith and her love for those beautiful children.

The Legacy of a SHEro

In 2017, my mother Lis died. I lost my best friend, and in some ways my world, since we did everything together. I lost my first SHEro and I am still grieving from the loss. Even though she is not physically here, I can still feel her energy and love surrounding me. I gained another angel. She is still empowering me and many other women, even from heaven.

My mother was a powerhouse. She went through a lot but never lost her beauty. Her grace and her generosity touched many lives. At House of Gaia, our nonprofit community center, my mother became the "Mother to All." The center is her legacy – as am I, since I am who I am because of her.

I am grateful for growing up with her unconditional love, for her forgiveness, for her smiles and hugs, and for everything she still represents to me. In my spiritual world, she guides me, she protects me, and she whispers words of encouragement. She tells me to go on, to live my life, and to be happy! Her spirit reminds me to shine, to self-regulate around food and work, to drink lots of water, to take long walks on the beach, and to dance!

The Power of Freedom

After my mother's death, my stepfather Roberto moved back to Brazil to be closer to his own family and I lost him in my daily life. My emotions were raw. I became sad and lonely, and my anxiety returned. Even simple tasks were difficult to handle.

I had to become my own SHEro.

By dedicating time to learning Positive Psychology, I shifted from negative emotions to more positive emotions in an upward spiral. I felt the power of freedom coming back, encouraging me to live again. Slowly, joy returned to my life.

To ground myself and return to balance, I practice the five aspects of SPIRE, a model of well-being created by Dr. Tal Ben-Shahar and Megan McDonough.

Spiritual: Living our purpose and mindfully savoring the present moment

Physical: Caring for and exercising the body; tapping into the mind-body-spirit connection

Intellectual: Engaging in deep learning; opening to experiences

Relational: Nurturing a constructive relationship with the self and others; fostering meaningful connections

Emotional: Feeling all emotions; reaching towards resilience and positivity

The SPIRE model ignited my spirit and filled me with hope. I have worked hard to recognize my roots, overcome my fears, grow from my traumas, and celebrate my strengths. Meditation, not medication, helped my spirit to be free, my mind to be clean, and my heart to be heard.

I am so grateful for my gifts in life:

- Mateus and his wisdom
- Adam and his unconditional love
- My global connections and my spiritual family
- My work with the universities and the nonprofit center
- My commitment to the Science of Happiness projects

Mateus has grown to be a wise man – he is an educator, an environmentalist, and in his own way, a philosopher. Our conversations are always so profound, providing much food for thought. I am proud to say that he is free to be his true self and live his authentic life. Mateus inspires me every day to be my own SHEro, as he is my hero. He is the joy of my life and my best teacher.

My husband Adam encourages me to be my authentic self; he is my supporter and cheerleader, as I am for him and his dreams.

My global community supports me – as I support them – in moments of both joy and need. In 2022, Suely (our director) and I started **Project Happiness** at House of Gaia, which is a highly customized coaching program for the autistic population and their families. At our center, we are committed to making many differences in this world and empowering as many individuals in need as we can, just like "Mother to All" did.

I have found the ability and wisdom to always return to the light, and the determination and courage to cross the darkness, despite challenges and fears.

I am committed to my journey of love, creativity and happiness, as my spirit is aligned with my choices, and my choices are aligned with my spirit.

My superpower is to empower others to cultivate their own SHEro mindset. As I and the other SHEroes in this book share our stories, we hope to inspire you to develop your own superpowers.

Seven Tips to Cultivate a SHEro Mindset

1. Take **care** of your body, mind and soul with **kindness**.
2. Focus on your **purpose**.
3. Listen and follow your **heart**.
4. Practice **compassion** and **forgiveness** for yourself and others.
5. **Be grateful** for ALL life lessons. In reality, nothing is bad if you are willing to explore different perspectives.
6. **Be of service** to others.
7. **Love** yourself unconditionally, **be authentic**, and embrace all of you!

The Flower of Life

Inspiration to Free Yourself

In life, we often focus on the verbs to do and to have, but *The SHEro Mindset* is about practicing the verb to BE. Use these affirmations to free yourself from what holds you back.

Be Vulnerable
Embrace vulnerability to set you free of fear. Stop letting secrets and shame color your stories. As we practice vulnerability with grace, we can move through life like the wind. Give yourself permission to exist, to feel and to express. Meditation can also free you of thoughts and judgment so you can connect with your higher self.

Be Safe
I like to say, "If you are not hurting yourself, others, or the environment, you can be whatever you want to be." I want to empower you to be you, but still be safe. You were born free and it is your responsibility to find out who you really are, not who your parents or society want you to be. Claim who you are, and others will feel safe around you. Live as your true self, and you will feel safe in the world.

Be Expressive
A child is free to scream, to cry, to laugh. As we grow older, we lose our natural ability to express who we are. We lose our spontaneity and instead try to please others, to be accepted or loved. You are beautiful, your flaws are beautiful, you are perfect as you are. All of the things we call mistakes are part of lessons to become our best selves. Express who you are.

The world is ready to experience you in all of your authentic beauty, but it can only do that if you express that beauty!

Be Authentic

Who are you at your core, underneath all the layers that you may have created to protect yourself? How can you experience your true self? When and how do you connect to your higher self? Can you take off the masks? Life can be short; how can you be free to be yourself? Live today like it is the first and the last day of your life. Let yourself be free!

Freedom Meditation

May all of us be free to pursue happiness...
genuine, authentic and whole
happiness that comes from deep inside of our souls...
happiness as a reflection of others' happiness...
without slavery, without oppression...
where peace prevails.

Truly serving our Purpose...
accepting our differences

Giving and receiving positive experiences
feeling a sense of belonging
and the importance of meaningful connections...

Co-creating...
our life according to true values
that promote order, growth and development
where we can feel safe emotionally,
physically and spiritually

With equal opportunities
for health and education
for clean water, air and food...

With a positive outcome for our children's future
for our humanity
for our nature
for our environment...
curating a life with more justice, inclusion and virtues

Healing... from inside and out
transforming, evolving, and seeking the light

The Power of
WISDOM

The virtue of Wisdom gives us perspective, helping us to make choices that give us a sense of peace and accomplishment. Being smart is not necessarily being wise. To be wise, one needs patience; sometimes, sacrifice and resilience. The goal of Wisdom is to cultivate long-term positive results. Using the power of Wisdom, one can benefit all of humanity and the life of our planet. Wisdom becomes a stronger virtue if integrated with the others.

Wisdom determines creativity, curiosity, judgment, love of learning and perspective. We can intentionally use these particular character strengths to cultivate greater wisdom in day-to-day choices.

PHOEBE ATKINSON

CHAPTER 2

Wisdom

Julia became my homeopathic doctor 21 years ago, in 2001. As a way of introducing her, I want to share the following letter that I wrote to her:

My Dear Julia,

I am so grateful that you became my homeopathic doctor when I was so sick and needed a compassionate doctor. When you and I met, I was going through a lot of emotional pain, trying to finalize my six-year divorce from Tarso. My health at the time was deteriorating, as I was diagnosed with asthma. Anxiety was dominating my life and I didn't even have enough air to walk to the bus stop to pick up Mateus.

At that time, Mateus was not doing well either. He had horrible bronchitis and sinusitis. Poor child, he would spend a week in bed with the curtains closed every time he became sick. I remember arriving in your office and looking at you. I saw a very wise woman in front of me. I immediately trusted you and felt very blessed to have you in our lives.

You took interest in my story and spent a lot of time with my son and me. At the time, it was so needed, and I felt heard. This is one of the greatest things any human can experience – to feel heard. But what matters the most was the time you spent trying to understand the real causes behind our illnesses. It felt like we mattered to you. Over the years, with the right treatment, we felt so much better and became vibrant. I became so healthy, and I had the energy I needed to expand my horizons and travel the world. Mateus had allergies, but now he works outdoors. He was inspired by you, and by your suggestion for him to join the Chewonki Foundation, since he has a love for nature. That suggestion for him to join the program in Maine was a life-changer for him.

I believe that our lives crossed each other's path for spiritual reasons. I needed to be healthy for motherhood, to expand my travel business, and to open the House of Gaia Nonprofit Center. Over these 21 years, we have shed tears together as we grieved the losses of our mothers. We also shared a good number of laughs and joy!

I know I can count on you, and you know you can count on me anytime. Our friendship turned into sisterhood, and it is so priceless. I pray for God to give you health, patience and wisdom to continue your mission on this earth as the best homeopathic doctor I have ever met. You are so special to our family; you are my SHEro and I hope I am yours.

LOVE YOU, LULU

Julia's Story
The Nature Within

Throughout my younger life and my earlier experiences, there was so much drama and trauma that happened to me personally. It felt like I had a lot of struggles, and the only way that I persevered was to be of service to others. I was a very sensitive, empathetic and kind child. I was raised in a situation where there was not only abuse, but emotional violence.

I remember being about 5 years old and it was the fall. The leaves were changing colors on the trees. We lived in a small town, Oak Lawn, a suburb outside of Chicago. It was still like Indian summer; it was hot.

I had learned in kindergarten about metamorphosis. I learned about an egg that grows into a larva, then a chrysalis, and finally emerges as a butterfly. I was so excited to have found caterpillars (what I believed to be caterpillars) inside of a garbage can. How magical it was to find those creatures in my own backyard.

I rushed into the house and grabbed my father's briefcase. It was the first thing I could find to move those little caterpillars. I took them and secretly put them in the briefcase. Afterward, I went to every tree, and I placed the little baby caterpillars on the trees. I was going to help them to become majestic butterflies. I was a child who believed in beauty and the process of transformation.

My father found out that what I'd been carrying in his briefcase were nothing but ugly maggots. He was very angry at me. I did not understand why; I thought I was doing something good – protecting the caterpillars and giving them a better home. I really wanted to save them from the life inside of a garbage can. My father could not believe what I had done. I did not know the "caterpillars" would become flies. But nevertheless, he yelled at me and punished me for my actions.

What could have been a teachable moment for a child turned into shame and made me feel ignorant, thoughtless, and sad. This story became a theme in my life. I was simply not allowed to genuinely express myself; to see the magic in life as a child.

Nature Felt Natural
From a young age, I have carried the weight of the world on my shoulders. Through life's experiences, I learned that I was someone who cared for people and the world around me. I was born an empath. I was a little blonde child with big blue eyes – full of wonder, trust and innocence.

Fear, hopelessness and shame became a part of me in my dysfunctional childhood. Slowly, I was losing my vitality, energy and my joy. I was turning into a sick child. I did not know how severe it was, and I was not given the help I needed.

My throat became inflamed as my body could not cope anymore with my challenges. My throat was the gatekeeper of my soul. The good thing was that my throat was protecting my entire body, so that it would not be contaminated. The bad thing was that my voice was suppressed and shut down. My health was deteriorating due to the overgrowth of strep; the situation lasted for many years. The pain was excruciating. Antibiotics became a way of life.

The SHEro's Childhood

I was constantly tired, and had little energy left to play and just be a child. Since I was the oldest girl child in my family, I assumed the role of the caregiver of my younger siblings by the time I was 9 years old. I had to overcome my own limitations to learn how to care for others. I did not rebel; instead, I embraced this new role.

And despite my health crises, I still found joy with my siblings. I was determined to keep them innocent and free, and to protect them from the bad things I had experienced, which I will not specifically name.

As I grew up, my body became strong, and I had the aptitude to be an athlete. I felt my strengths growing each day and my wings started to spread more and more. I was becoming my own SHEro. Team sports gave me confidence and became a tool for exercising my powers. Those were good days. I was morphing into my own butterfly.

I was lucky enough to be invited by my school to travel with other students for a wildlife immersion program in Canada. That was a pivotal experience in my life, where I found my first passion: to learn to live in harmony with nature! In nature, I could be myself; I felt safe. In the wilderness, I was home. I invited my inner child to be expressive, daring, and playful again. Those five weeks were transformative for me. I went back home feeling like a hero and ready to live my life.

Falling in Love with Life

At the time I was finishing high school and starting college, I had a subscription to Backpacker magazine. I saw an ad for a camp counselor for a Jewish girls' camp. I immediately visualized myself working in the woods of Maine; I applied for the job, and after a week I was hired. At 18, I boarded a bus and traveled across the country. My destination was Monmouth, Maine.

I spent an amazing summer as the water skiing instructor and assistant trip leader. We took the campers on wilderness trips on the Appalachian Trail. It was an unforgettable time and I fell in love with life.

After the summer, I went back to Illinois State University. I knew in my heart that I wanted to study natural resource management and biology. During college, I integrated my love of nature with my academics, and I felt in control of my life. During that time of college, I was living independently, and I looked forward to visiting with my younger siblings.

When I graduated, I took a job in New Hampshire as a wildlife rehabilitator and as an intern for a science center. It was a true dream job for a nature lover! I lived on the land, I took care of the animals, and I taught educational programs for the students. It was such a rich experience, and I celebrated my 21st birthday there.

The Mother of the Wild

While I was working at the science center in New Hampshire we rescued a tiny beaver. He was the size of a shoe, so cute, so light, and so vulnerable. I became the caregiver of this baby. Later I found out the backstory: hunters had blown up the dam and the mother had been killed.

The little baby beaver went everywhere with me. I would tuck him into my shirt at night to go to sleep because he wanted to be close to me. I was his mom and all that he had. Eventually it was released back into the wild. I was the mother of the wild one. It felt good and right to take care of the animals.

Life was taking twists and turns, and I found my way back to Maine. I felt ready to start my own business and I became an entrepreneur at the age of 25. I have so many good memories from that time. I was teaching children about the environment, in costume, in the public school system. I was so playful and creative. I even had a butterfly costume to help the children to develop a love of learning. I had freedom to share what I knew about nature.

A Wise Woman

Even though things were going well in my life, I still suffered from strep throat. I decided to take charge of my health and consulted a specialist in Boston about my chronic illness.

He said to me, "Your tonsils are the worst tonsils I've ever seen. You have a huge infection, and they must come out."

I said, "I would consider the surgery under one circumstance. I want you to explain where the infection will lodge in my body when it no longer has my tonsils." I knew that the tonsils were the first line of defense for my immune system. I felt angry at him.

He said, "You are being ridiculous."

I said, "No, I'm not being ridiculous; if you can answer the question to my satisfaction, I'll consider the surgery."

He basically told me to leave his office, and I left. I went back home, feeling dismissed by the doctor. I knew I had to do something and be wise with my choices.

It was 1989 and I was not in a good space. I had to address my emotional and physical health. I was in a crisis, but I would soon meet my spiritual guide, healer, and therapist. She was truly a wise woman, who later would become my colleague, friend, and ally.

She asked if I had ever considered homeopathic treatment. I knew a little bit about homeopathy, but I thought, *Come on. I am a scientist. I'm rational and homeopathy doesn't make any sense to me. This is ridiculous, it's not real... they give you a placebo.*

She said in a gentle way, "Julia, do you trust me? I treat my entire family and myself with homeopathy. Why don't you just try it?"

I paused, took a deep breath, and answered her, "Well, I suppose I've got nothing to lose."

She was the answer to my prayers — my SHEro Denise. Now I had to exercise my own wisdom, and really follow through with her guidance for my cure.

I went for a consultation with the doctor that Denise recommended. I felt incredibly vulnerable, raw, and exposed. The doctor asked me a lot of questions; a lot about my history. It was like he could scan my entire body, mind, and soul. It was extremely uncomfortable. This was a man questioning me, poking and prodding into the private areas of my life.

I thought, *Whatever you're going to give me, it's not going to work.* What I thought I needed after the consultation was grape soda and Hostess cupcakes, and to be wrapped in a warm blanket. That was what comforted me as a child.

One week later, I received my remedy. It was just one dose, one time. I could not believe that after that, I never had strep throat again. I was grateful for the opportunity to experience homeopathy and for being brave.

Becoming a Healer

I was so impressed with the process of working with my wise healer and with the homeopathic treatment that had changed my life. I felt healthy again. My journey to become a healer had begun. In those days, there wasn't much homeopathic training in the USA, so I started gathering books and reading everything I could get my hands on about homeopathy.

I was still involved with wildlife as a wildlife rehabilitator. People knew about my skills, and they would bring injured animals to my front door. The wounded animals became my first patients. One time, a little owl was brought to me, and I will never forget how homeopathy healed his broken wing.

I was getting ready to close my business as an educator. I really wanted to study homeopathy and I wanted to be somewhere where it would be legal for me to practice homeopathy. I believe that in life, we are granted many possibilities to share our gifts. To become a healer would be fulfilling my purpose.

From 1992 to 1996, I was enrolled in a school in Florida where I learned acupuncture and became a doctor of oriental medicine. On the weekends, I studied homeopathy with a master of homeopathy.

From Outdoors to Indoors

For five years, I never saw the sun in Florida. I was up before it was light, and I was in class until 10 p.m. That was a big change in my life, which required many sacrifices. There was no question in my mind that I was on the right career path. I wanted people to feel heard. I chose to work with classical homeopathy and acupuncture, bringing balance to the body, mind and spirit.

In my practice, I want to deeply understand my patients. However, I don't want them to feel unsafe or exposed, as I did during my first consultation.

As an empath, I welcome my patients with kindness and compassion. I hold sacred space for people to tell their stories. People come in like a ball of yarn, and I have to pick and pull until I can find the single strand that will unravel that ball and smooth out all the edges. I found my joy in nature, but my passion is helping people to navigate their own way through the world.

The Tunnel of Light

Another event was about to change my life once again. For almost a week, I felt very sick with severe abdominal pain. I was alone, in bed, suffering in silence. The situation got progressively worse until I experienced a very high fever spike. When I arrived at the hospital, I told the nurse that I was in excruciating pain, even though outwardly I was stoic. This led to several hours of waiting before they brought me in for an abdominal CT scan.

The doctors discovered that I had numerous perforations, or holes, in my colon. They said that, in my situation, the condition could be managed with inpatient care using IV fluids and high-dose antibiotics. I would also need to have laparoscopic surgery within 72 hours to repair my damaged colon.

The next morning, the nurse misread my chart and gave me a heavy dose of morphine. I am highly allergic to that medication. Within seconds of it entering my bloodstream, the lower 28 inches of my intestines ruptured. I was screaming in agony from the pain.

Another CT scan was performed. The surgeon came into my room to explain that I had perforated diverticulitis and septicemia, and that I had to have emergency surgery to remove the damaged area of the colon.

As they wheeled me into surgery, the surgeon told me that I would survive the surgery but my chances of surviving the sepsis was 50/50 at best. I broke into tears and kept repeating, "I am not ready." The surgeon told me that I didn't have a choice, and that if I didn't have surgery, I would die.

I was in surgery for six hours. They left my abdomen open because of the sepsis, inserted a drain, and attached a wound VAC (a suction pump to drain the infection). During the surgery, I stopped breathing. They shocked my heart, but I literally died on the surgery table on August 1, 2008.

It's true what they say about seeing a white light. For me, I was in a mist-covered, milky-white, tree-lined corridor, slowly walking forward. Everything appeared like cobwebs or cotton candy. I came to the end of the corridor, which I understood to be heaven. Immediately, I was slammed back into my body and away from the light. I felt God saying to me that it was not my time to go.

This experience happened again at least three or four times in the recovery room. My spirit was trying to leave my body, yet I was forced to stay. I was severely depressed, and I didn't want to be alive. At the time, I was angry with God that I survived the surgery. I thought, How could God let me get so close and then push me back into this world? I was done... in my life, in everything.

I felt that I had experienced enough joy and beauty; I traveled a lot; I had become a partner and stepmother, and had helped many patients. I had made true friends and I was ready for heaven.

The Nurse's Compassion

But, God had other plans for me. During my stay in the ICU, and despite my sorrow, I found kindness, compassion, and beauty. One nurse, a Russian woman, spoke to me on the first day after my surgery, when I was conscious. She asked me what she could do to make me comfortable.

I said, "You need to know me; I'm very private, very modest. I don't like to feel sweaty or dirty from the medication."

She nodded and said, "I will give you a sponge bath every day you are here."

In 2008, this was no longer a service provided in hospitals. This woman, this nurse, literally bathed me like a baby with tenderness, while preserving my dignity. She was my own personal angel. She even came into the hospital to bathe me on her days off. I will never forget that.

When I was in the recovery room after surgery, my colleague and friend, Dr. Anderson, had called my homeopathic doctor in Belgium. She explained what had happened and Dr. Henny prescribed the right homeopathic remedy.

I had been told I would have the wound VAC and an open wound for three to six months. But I recovered much more rapidly than the average patient. I underwent a second surgery on day 14 to close my wound, because I was healing so quickly from the inside out.

My Reason To Be Alive

Five months after the surgeries, I received a call from Ann Jerome, who runs the Academy of Classical Homeopathy (ACH). She wanted me to teach a long weekend in Florida. I didn't know if I was ready, so I told her I was weak and needed extra care. I didn't know my limits; I didn't want to overdo it. I told her that I needed to be treated like a child – to be fed good food, to be brought tea, and to be encouraged to take breaks, among other things.

Ann is an incredibly nurturing person and friend, and said that she could do all those things. So, off to Florida I went.

What a long way I had come from where I had been five months before – lying in my bed, stoic, not asking for help until I almost died.

I didn't really want to go to Florida, as I was having a real crisis of faith. I no longer understood my purpose, my value, or why I had survived. I truly felt that life was too painful, too full of suffering.

However, the teaching in Florida turned out to be – without question – the best teaching I had ever done. It flowed out of me, almost effortlessly. I know that the teaching came directly from God, Mother Mary, and all my angels and guides. Somehow, all I had experienced had made me a better teacher.

My students were awestruck and inspired. On my flight home, as I was basking in the magic of the weekend, it hit me – I had rediscovered my purpose. God was not done with me yet. I still had so much more to give. I survived and would thrive... I would be of service to others; I would shine my light and share my knowledge and my gifts with my students, my patients, and all whom I would encounter.

Service to Myself and to Others

We as women are trained to believe that it's not acceptable to take care of ourselves. We're supposed to take care of everyone else. I know my wisdom has changed and helped many patients. While there are things that I do that keep me on the path of wellness, I don't think I've ever really learned the skills of self-care.

The SHEro Mindset

My SHEro Denise, as my constant guide, encourages me to take care of myself first before serving others. Everyone should have a SHEro like this in their life.

The experience of almost dying helped me to see that my purpose is to understand the importance of self-love and self-care for myself and for others. When I am in service, I feel present, and it takes me out of the darkness. It brings me into the light. It brings me joy!

My work is to understand people's stories, sharing in the depth of our connection. I can very easily walk in their shoes and understand their struggles, because I struggle too. So, I can act as a guide, and I can dispense homeopathic remedies. I can use my acupuncture needles too. But what my patients value most is the experience of being with me in communion. Patients feel validated and are given the skills and the health to go out into the world.

I like to visualize that I wrap my clients in the softest, warmest blankets possible. When they're ready to face the world again, they know that they have protection around them, and they are comforted and safe.

God Grant Us the Wisdom

During our lives we will all be challenged; we will have to confront situations out of our control. We will have the opportunity to act wisely and bravely. Sometimes we simply have to pause, refrain from acting impulsively, and conscientiously make a wise decision. We should not be carried away by our triggers, negative thoughts, emotions, or fears. Certainly, nature is here to teach us how to be wiser. We can always learn a valuable lesson from Mother Nature. She never remains the same; she adjusts to survive.

As for me, I had to accept that I will not determine when it is time for me to leave this earth. God has given me the wisdom to understand my limitations, to overcome my past traumas, and to be resilient above and beyond what I thought I could be. I understand my purpose in life, and I encourage you to also pursue your dreams and your purpose.

Our health will be determined by how aligned and balanced we are in our mind, body, and spirit. Therefore, I will continue my journey of love, joy and compassion to serve as long as I breathe.

My wish for you is to seek help in times of need, and don't settle for any help until you find the right help. Just remind yourself from time to time that you are not walking alone in life. There are people truly serving, guided by their hearts, and sincere in their wish to help. These are the angels among us.

— DR. JULIA A. EASTMAN

Inspiration to Cultivate Wisdom

In life, we often focus on the verbs to do and to have, but *The SHEro Mindset* is about practicing the verb to BE. Use these suggestions to cultivate the wisdom of the SHEro.

Be Honest

Finding clarity is the first step on the path of wisdom. You have to use your wisdom to clarify what you need, what you want, and how much energy you are willing to put into the work of developing and healing yourself. To be honest with yourself, write in your journal, create a vision board, and ask for help. I know you are wise. I encourage you to dive deeply into your own self to curate the life you want to live. This can only happen with honesty.

Be Kind

We can empower each other with the wisdom of kindness. Yes, a kind person is very wise. They understand the need of another to be heard, to be accepted, to be seen, and to be included. When we are kind, we embody wisdom for ourselves and for others.

Be Intuitive

A wise person listens to their intuition. This can be found through one's third eye, and the "gut" or solar plexus. The ancients believed that our consciousness resides in our upper belly, which has been called our second brain. Wisdom comes from your spiritual connection with, and your intuitive understanding of, this world we live in. Use your intuition – the more you use it, the stronger it becomes.

Be Aware
Pay attention to your body – be aware of any pain or discomfort. Sit with your sensations and listen to what they are telling you. What sensations are here to guide you? Which ones are trying to distract you? Awareness helps us to have the wisdom to separate the light from the dark.

Be Perseverant
The path of wisdom will require perseverance. In order to change, we will need to get out of our comfort zone and push through the natural resistance that we create. Life is not going to be easy or fun all the time. However, procrastination is not going to help us either. Every day, we focus on our dreams, goals and achievements. And every day, we endure the difficulties with peace in our hearts. We do the work, and we persevere. This is how we embody Wisdom.

Be the one to shine. Be your own healer; use your Wisdom, and make choices that will allow you to find true happiness.

Wisdom Meditation

Start your day by opening your eyes,
being kind to yourself, and being grateful for life!
You may be facing the most difficult time
You may be lost
You may be frightened
Remember, this moment shall pass
Take a deep breath... feel the love that surrounds you
Given by the trees, by the bees, by the sun, by the birds
An unconditional love that comes from heaven
You are loved
Even when things are chaotic
You are beautiful
Have courage to make the changes to make yourself happier
To make yourself healthier, to make yourself whole
Have the wisdom to find peace
To share peace and to be part of a harmonious world
End your day by closing your eyes and being grateful for life!
And during the time you are asleep – rejuvenate, regenerate,
recuperate. Let the wisdom of your mind, body and soul
reset, wake and heal you.

The Power of
JOY

Joy is different from happiness. One can find joy in the most difficult time of life by being grateful for simple acts of kindness, by finding beauty in every moment, by being genuine about loving and by exchanging positive energy. Without Joy, the world would be flat and raw. Joy adds colors and shapes to our lives, and enables us to unleash authentic happiness.

*Drop down and back, opening to the
quiet joy that emerges from your heart.
Be in this amazing journey called life,
flowing with unexpected twists and turns,
connecting with joy even during the
hardest times.*

MEGAN MCDONOUGH

CHAPTER 3

Joy

The first time I met Evonn was at the open house party for House of Gaia. She had been invited by a friend; I soon became curious about her. The way she carried herself was impressive, and her confidence was powerful beyond words. One could feel her energy from a distance; she definitely stood out in the crowd.

Later, Evonn came to check out our programs for her young children. And I also organized a beautiful princess party for her youngest daughter.

During the last 13 years at House of Gaia, I have seen many sides of Evonn. However, her biggest role is the joyful parent.

Evonn is very energetic and creative. She likes to come to our nonprofit and volunteer with her family at our social inclusion programs. I can guarantee that when she arrives at the center, she will be a ball of joy!

However, like the other SHEroes, Evonn has a story to share. One time, she came to me and opened her heart. She told me about a tragic part of her life that shocked me. How could a person so full of joy have suffered so much?

The SHEro Mindset

A part of our center's curriculum is to spread joy. And Evonn, despite her tragedy, became one of my SHEroes as she helped us fulfill our mission. Her mindset is to overcome negative emotions and transform them into positive emotions, and doing that became part of my mindset too. Thanks to people like Evonn, who is a true role model, our nonprofit's curriculum is filled with joyful experiences.

— LULU

Evonn's Story
Lessons of the Divine

I was born in Germany and lived there on and off for most of my childhood. Monika and Roy, my parents, met at a swimming pool in Homburg, Germany. My father was born in Manchester, England, but because of his mother's marriage to an American officer – and fate – he was in the U.S. Army and stationed in Miesau, Germany. My mother was a young German girl that lived in Lambsborn, one of the nearby villages.

We moved back and forth to the United States, and on each return, we lived in a different part of Germany. My parents were young, and did the best they could with what they thought they knew as they navigated parenthood and marriage.

As a child, I found my joy in the fields and woods that surrounded my grandparents' house in Lambsborn. I spent most weekends, summers, and all school holidays with my Oma and Opa. Lambsborn was a community of older people; the only other children there were other families' grandchildren who came for occasional visits.

My days were spent exploring the woods that surrounded that small village, building forts, and visiting neighbors for a conversation or a sewing lesson. Oma and Opa's house rules were simple:

The SHEro Mindset

1. Be home to eat when the church bell rings at 12 p.m. and at 6 p.m.
2. No yodeling in the tree stands because it echoes (I sounded like a wounded cat).
3. Don't run up and down the stairs in wooden clogs during nap time.
4. No worms allowed at the table.

I followed the rules, most of the time. I was a bit of a prankster, which occasionally did get me into trouble. I was an only child who spent most of my time alone. My only steady companion for a couple of years was a dog named Maggie – a fox terrier rescue who was grateful, like I was, to have a friend. Maggie taught me about love, affection and responsibility, and giving her up when we left Germany was my first heartache. I still have a photo of her on my dresser. That photo reminds me that inside, I am still that young girl – full of joy, hope and adventure.

When I am asked where home is, I always think of my grandparents' house and that tiny village of Lambsborn.

The Front Row

Because of frequent moves and new schools, I didn't really fit into one clique or group at school, but floated in and out of every group. I adapted to most situations and was open to new beginnings, but friendships were hard to leave behind. I became aware at an early age that change and loss are a part of everyday living.

When I was 10 years old, my mother left and rarely looked back. My father became my only parent until he married Janet. Together, the three of us moved back to the United States, when I was 13 years old.

The Art of Listening

My father taught me to be quiet and listen. I enjoyed the company of adults and was able to hold my own in conversations without acting foolish, at least most of the time. I became an observer, a people-watcher; I could read body language and pick up on the small things that people did not say. This life lesson of being a good listener helped me value actions over words, and to read between the lines in both the business and personal arenas.

My mother and I reconnected when I was about 15 and I moved back to live with her just before my father was assigned to Korea. Mom had remarried and was living in Myrtle Beach, South Carolina. By the age of 16, my independent nature and turbulent home life led me to pursue new adventures on my own. I was emancipated, which meant I could legally be considered an adult. My high school chorus teacher inspired me to enter competitions, and later to audition for placement in a school for performing arts in Atlanta, Georgia. Flowing creative energy brought me joy, and music became a gateway to self-expression and inner peace. That is also when I started working and learning the fine art of survival.

I lived on my own in an apartment with not much more than a chair and a bed, but I loved it. A stray dog found me and once again I had a faithful, loving companion. My mother would send me "care packages" of toilet paper, macaroni and cheese, and ramen noodles. My adventures encouraged me to grow up quickly and to learn the ways of the world from the front row. I look back on those times fondly, and I believe I was gifted with resourcefulness and a positive attitude, which made the bumps and bruises easier.

The Chosen Stories

When Lulu called and asked me to share my story, I immediately said yes. I did not hesitate or think twice. I have learned a lot of lessons in this journey called life, and I was ready to share them. I am honored that Lulu chose me to represent the virtue of Joy in this book. I believe Joy is a soulful collaboration from spirit to spirit, and that we are most connected to people and nature when we experience Joy.

I believe that our life is a series of befores-and-afters; in an instant, you and your life will never be the same. I will share two events that impacted, changed and transformed my life. This is the first story.

My Children, My Life

In 1995, my daughter Sarina turned 1 and my son Julian was born. They are my "Irish twins." Destin was 8 and Hannah was 5, and we lived in the Poconos in a lake resort community near a small town with one traffic light. My husband Scot commuted into New York City three days a week. We were in the art business and were surrounded by beauty and nature. Weekends were spent exploring and spending time together. There was ice skating in the winter, and pony rides and walks in the summer.

After a year in the Poconos, we had an incredible opportunity to open another gallery/showroom, in Atlanta, Georgia inside the Design Center. It was an open concept, with full staff. That meant we didn't have to be there or have our own staff to man the gallery. My husband could still travel to New York and Los Angeles, where we were in partnership with Scot's brothers. Atlanta had always held such a special place in my heart and I thought it would be the perfect place to raise our children. The opportunity was a blessing.

New beginnings and moving was never a problem for me or for Scot, who grew up living overseas and spoke five languages fluently. My husband and I shared a love of adventure and creating new opportunities. We both looked at this new opportunity to establish a home base.

We found a lovely three-story home just outside of Atlanta and made the move at the beginning of summer. I remember feeling like I could live there for the rest of my life. I was happy and fulfilled. My older children were doing so well with the move, and my babies Sarina and Julian were pure joy.

What I didn't know was that a few weeks after moving there, my world would turn upside down. I have come to believe that bad things tend to happen fast, and will hit you when you least expect it, in ways you can never imagine.

More Than a Tragic Story

I mostly worked from home and would handle the details for the gallery openings and artist shows. The new space in the design center was almost complete, and my husband and I were preparing for the opening show.

We had an au pair who came with us from the Poconos to help us with the youngest children. Sarina was almost 15 months old and Julian was 11 weeks. My oldest daughter Destin was visiting my dad and Janet in Germany, and Hannah was visiting her father in Florida.

I came home from the gallery on an evening like any other that week. I had been at the gallery for the last three days, preparing for the opening of a show the following day. I was looking forward to being back at home with the children, unpacking our belongings and starting our new life. Little did I know...

That night, I brought home some salads for dinner and arrived home after dark. Baby Julian was sitting in his bouncy chair in the living room. The sitter told me that Sarina was in bed asleep upstairs. I completed a few chores, and went to check on her and give her a goodnight kiss.

As I got closer to her, I saw that she was covered up with a heavy hand-knitted blanket – which was odd to me, as it was so hot. I took the blanket off of her, and leaned over to give her a kiss. I knew at that moment that my precious little one's spirit was gone.

I carried her quickly downstairs, began CPR and called 911.

Once the ambulance and police arrived, our little girl was taken to the hospital. My husband and I followed behind in a police car. At the hospital, we were taken to a small empty room for hours and we realized that the door was locked. They, the hospital staff and the police, thought the unthinkable: one of us must have killed our daughter. They wouldn't let us see her, and the words they spoke to us that night haunted me.

We were so broken and lost. I kept reliving that day and that night, over and over, moment by moment. I agonized over the many tiny things I wished I could have changed. I remembered signs that indicated that I should have stayed home, like forgetting my gallery keys; having to return home twice to retrieve a security pass; seeing an accident on the highway; almost running out of gas, and other little things that I would later recognize as Divine.

It would take days before the authorities determined that we didn't kill our Sarina and that we weren't home when she died. For 10 days, my son Julian was cared for in the foster care system. We were only allowed to see him – under watchful eyes – every couple of days.

Our home was located just outside of the Atlanta jurisdiction and the case was handled by an adjacent small town in a rural county. Although the investigation released us from the suspicion of causing Sarina's death, the fight to prove that we were good, loving and caring parents had just started. In the eyes of the prosecutor, we were still the bad parents who had hired the au pair. He even told me that if I had stayed home like a "good wife," my daughter would still be alive.

I was so paralyzed by the weight of guilt and the anguish of losing our sweet little girl that I couldn't leave our house or even the bedroom. My husband couldn't be anywhere close to home. We grieved separately and alone. The blur of those days and weeks that followed was as if I was frozen in shock and encapsulated with grief. I couldn't function and needed help. So, I went to live with my family in Germany. My husband went to Los Angeles to be with his brothers.

The after began for both of us. The prosecutors' case against our sitter took two years to bring to court. During those two years, many details were uncovered about our sitter's history of violence, along with the many lies that she and her mother had told us. We were told she was 15 when we met her, and we even celebrated her 16th birthday. We later learned she was only 14. Her diabetic health condition was even kept from us for a time, until we traveled overnight with her.

We knew Candy as a teenager in the Poconos who helped her mother with an in-home child care center. She had helped us with the children for over a year before we moved to Atlanta.

She would even stay with us on school holidays, and would come over to play with the girls or go to family outings. I was pregnant with Julian then, and welcomed the help. The girls enjoyed her company; she always arrived with a backpack filled with games and treasures. I felt like she was part of the family.

When we decided to move to Atlanta, it was her mother who called and suggested she could come with us for the summer, with a plan for her to return home in mid-July.

The week before Sarina was killed, I had taken Candy to see the Fourth of July fireworks, while my husband stayed home with the little ones. She asked me if she could stay with us; to live with us in Atlanta. I told her no, but that she was welcome to visit often and come during her school holidays, if her mother would agree. I wondered later if that conversation caused her to come up with what we would later learn was a plan to take our son Julian and run away. That night, if I hadn't gone to check on Sarina, to kiss her, I wouldn't have discovered that she had already left us. Candy had already packed a bag with clothing, food and diapers. She would have taken my 3-month-old son Julian and left while my husband and I slept.

Candy was prosecuted as an adult, and received a sentence of 25 years to life. The details of my daughter's last day and the extent of her injuries were unbearable to hear and imagine. We believed that Candy deserved to spend every minute of the rest of her life in prison for doing that kind of evil.

The SHEro Mindset

Just the year before, a state law was changed so that 95 percent of a sentence would have to be served. So, she remained in jail for 19 years. Without that law change, she would have been free in just four to six years. After release, Candy moved back to the Poconos and lived there until she passed away due to diabetes.

We Lost Our World

I can't quite describe the emotions I felt. My baby was not there anymore. I think I died that night; part of my soul had left with her. I could not function. I needed medication for pretty much everything – to sleep, to eat, to stay awake. I had nightmares and unyielding flashbacks. I was a crippled zombie.

I struggled to even breathe, let alone take care of three children. My Dad and Janet were incredible; they helped keep us together. Day by day, minute by minute, we moved forward. My husband Scot decided it would be better for him to go to Los Angeles for healing and work, so he could support us financially. We had planned for him to join us overseas, but that wasn't in the cards for us. We divorced a year later, soon after my parents, children and I moved to England.

My children and my parents helped me to survive. I found strength in simple daily activities with my children, such as feeding them, taking them to school, and reading and coloring with them. The medications helped some, but I had it in my head that Sarina was all alone and that I needed to be with her. In one of my darker moments, I attempted to kill myself while my children were away for the weekend. I was discovered and saved by a fluke visit from a friend, and taken to the hospital. I believe after waking up a few days later in the hospital, I felt that I had no choice but do something different.

Later, I had a very lucid encounter with my daughter's spirit in a dream. Afterward, I can only describe the shift inside me as a movement from thinking to awareness and from believing to knowing. An awakening to purpose. It was an awareness that I was not my thoughts, that I could create a space – even if small – to observe. I discovered that my thoughts were faulty, even in the best circumstances. I realized that if I kept listening to and believing my thoughts, I would miss the deeper perfection in the moment that is always already here. I also became aware that thinking wasn't going to heal me; only through being and feeling would I be able to experience joy and start living again.

Grace and Divine Order

When you lose a child, you join an exclusive club that no one ever wants to belong to. In an instant, you have everything in common with people who you wouldn't normally have anything in common with. Then, you also have absolutely nothing in common with your closest family and friends with whom you used to share everything. I became acutely aware that everything I had ever been, or had identified with, was suddenly gone.

I was told that grief is a process, and you go through five emotional stages: denial, anger, bargaining, depression, and finally acceptance. I'm not sure I ever went through those stages. Certainly not in the order you are "supposed" to. My experience is that grief is something you carry with you wherever you go. Some days the load is heavier; other days it is less so, but it is always there. There is no getting over it or through it. It is endured.

Perspective

Events, especially tragic and painful ones, create memories that are painted with emotion, and then they are cataloged and filed in our consciousness or subconscious. The emotions we attach to events are often different for each person experiencing the same event. The moment we rise above mere survival, the question of meaning and purpose becomes of paramount importance in life. Our experience – and memory of the experience – is shaped by our beliefs, emotions and perspectives.

Feeling Heard

It is through the process of being (not doing), and sharing our feelings and our unique experiences that we begin to feel a little lighter. We are able to breathe a bit deeper and take another step forward.

Healing

I believe we endure suffering when we focus inward and on ourselves. But when we focus outward on others, we can develop deep understanding and empathy. Through this process, we may be able to find grace and our own healing.

A Moment of Clarity

I realized that I was either going to continue to spiral downward or figure out a way to make what happened to my beautiful little girl mean something – beyond the tragedy. It was a moment of choice. I realized I had to either choose consciously or react unconsciously.

My choice was also to live – for myself and for my other children. I chose to integrate Sarina's spirit and joy into all areas of our lives. I then began to ask my inner true self and the Divine for guidance: How do I have my daughter's legacy be more than a tragic story in a headline? How can I celebrate her and help others to protect their children from such a tragedy? What can I give here from where I am; how can I be of service?

A clear understanding came to me, and I realized that I could not receive what I was unable to give. Love, peace, joy, understanding and compassion all come to us when we give them or express them. I realized they needed to be given to myself and others if I were to create an extraordinary life. That is really where the glimmer of my hope and healing began.

As my awareness changed, I started to shift my mindset. I came to realize that events in our life are unstable and constantly changing and therefore we cannot attach to them. True happiness and joy cannot be built on something unstable. It has to come from within.

The Steps I Took To Rediscover My Joy: P-H-G

Purpose – I found my purpose and meaning not simply by "doing," but by bringing forth a state of consciousness and light wherever I am.

Healing – I healed through giving and being of service.

Gratitude – I chose to live in gratitude and allowed myself to find joy in all moments, especially in the most challenging ones.

Connections Through Joy

My family and I discovered that Sarina is with us every moment of every day. Her light helps me find my way when I am lost or can't feel my way forward. It is through joy that I can be intimately connected to my daughter's spirit. During the most joyful moments, I feel her deeply alive inside and around me. Joy is not something that can be given, but it can be shared. I believe that this internal state of being is the only true form of happiness.

Dragonfly Effects

Love never ends, love never dies. Some of us find meaningful signs that indicate our departed loved one's presence in our lives. The things that keep connecting us to our loved ones appear, and give us hope that our loved ones are well. I believe

Joy

that they send us messages: butterflies, cardinals, blue jays, feathers, or a sparkly piece of glitter.

My family found our messages in dragonflies. A dragonfly is a symbol of change, transformation and self-realization. It teaches us to love life, to rejoice and have faith, even during difficulties. At every major family event or milestone, a dragonfly will find us.

A perfect example was my daughter Hannah's high school graduation in Palm Beach. The event was held inside a convention center and was filled with people. As we were sitting and waiting to see and celebrate her, a colorful dragonfly came by, fluttering its long wings. It paused with us for some time, landing on my shoulder. In that instant, my heart became full, and I knew and felt our sweet pea Sarina's presence. I thought, *She is sharing in this joyful occasion*!

After the ceremony, Hannah told us a dragonfly also came to visit her while she was on stage awaiting her diploma. That only confirmed my feelings. We were so overcome with emotion and gratitude.

Extraordinary moments of connection can and do happen every day. We just need to have our hearts open to experience them. Be open and aware.

Cultivating a Positive Mindset and Perspective

March 18, 2021 was another important "after" that altered my life. In retrospect, that morning, everything was screaming,

"Pay attention!" I woke up an hour earlier than usual. I decided to go to my fitness class at 7:30 a.m., instead of my usual 8:30 a.m. After a personal best class, I felt strong and incredibly happy. I jumped into the car and noticed the gas light was on. Remembering that it might have been on the day before, I knew I needed to gas up.

The gas station that I usually went to was blocked by unyielding cars. I ended up at a gas station that I didn't usually use because it was on the other side of a U-turn. I pulled up to the pump, got out and scanned my card, but the sale wouldn't go through. I thought, That is strange, I know there is money in there. I sat back down in my car to check my debit card balance. The bank app wouldn't load. Everything was challenging...

I found some cash and went inside to pay for gas. I walked through the double doors into the store and I noticed a man. He was agitated and seemed very upset. He bumped into me on his way out. I could literally feel his anger. I could hear my friend Cristy's voice in my head: Just a soul in need of love. That was the thought I shifted to.

After I prepaid for the gasoline, I headed back out toward my car. But I didn't realize that the agitated man was now in his Jeep. For whatever reason, a few moments after I walked past him on my way to the pump, he decided to punch his vehicle into reverse. He accelerated very quickly, and he hit me. Everything happened so quickly, but it felt like slow-motion.

I was dazed, but I knew I had been hit by a car. As I laid in that parking lot, I began to assess myself: I was alive, all limbs seemed intact, and I could feel and move all my extremities.

As I pictured it in slow-motion memory, it seemed to be a graceful fall and I had even protected myself in the way I landed... at least, that is what I thought. Incredibly, an emergency room doctor who saw what had happened ran up to me and said, "Let me help you." I relaxed a bit. I was so grateful that there was someone there for me – a real doctor.

Trying to Make Sense

While I lay there waiting for the ambulance, still slightly disoriented and with pain starting to creep in, I called my husband from my Apple watch. That way, he could listen in on what was happening as he made his way to me. I overheard the police officers questioning the driver. The driver explained about the fight he had been having with his girlfriend. He had gone inside the store looking for her just before getting into his car, and he had planned on reversing into a lane to gas up. He was very shaken and full of remorse.

Now surrounded by first responders, I felt very present, aware and calm. I began to think that there must be a reason that the accident occurred. I immediately tried to piece together what had just happened to find the reason for divine intervention. Maybe when the angry man hit me, it kept him off the road. Perhaps his girlfriend or another driver was saved by him hitting me instead. Did he need this moment of grace?

If he had not hit me, would he have hit someone else? The ER doctor? Maybe the doctor had somebody to save that day. Maybe the woman getting in her car needed a delay.

All I knew was: all is Divine. I didn't need to challenge the reason. I needed to surrender and have faith.

Six Inches

When I watched the video of the accident, I saw how hard I had been hit. My body was tossed in the air and spun around, my legs went up in the air over my head, and I had hit my head on the pavement. It was not as I pictured it before; it was not a casual accident and I was not graceful by any means. The car that hit me had backed up very quickly.

Had I been six inches to the left, my head and entire body would have been directly under his rear tire, and I might not be alive. I am so very grateful, with a heart full of love and joy, to have more moments with my loved ones.

It's been almost a year now. I do have a traumatic brain injury which makes some things more challenging; but it brings me an awareness to be kind to myself. Some days, I walk with a cane; other days, I don't need to. I know without a doubt that this experience, all of it, has changed me for the better. I am more present and kinder to my body, and I am grateful for every moment.

Positive Mindset

It's interesting when we allow the divine order to speak a little louder than our reason. The divine energy appears in everything we do and everything we are. In every single moment, you can experience the miracle of life – that positive mindset, or as Lulu calls it, the SHEro mindset. It is the shift to not allowing your thoughts to dictate your experience.

Sometimes events or tragedy can trigger such a shift of awareness, but it is still a process – and once started, it influences everything we do. It becomes integrated into our everyday lives, so instead of being lost or trapped in our patterns of thinking, we become awake to the awareness behind it. This gives us the courage to thrive instead of just surviving.

Divine Intervention

As I grow older, I am better at retaining a positive SHEro mindset, and quicker at moving into that awareness. I know that I can experience challenge, loss, and even tragedy, and still make the choice to accept the flow of life and the divine order of things. I find grace, gratitude and Joy.

My Joy

My life is blessed with extraordinary love, help and support from my friends and family. Together, we will always celebrate Sarina and the precious time we had with her. Her energy of pure joy inspires me to have gratitude for all moments, even the ones I don't wish for.

My children and I moved to southwest Florida from England in 2000. In 2005, I had another baby girl; her name is Tea. She is my miracle child. I remarried, to a wonderful man. Andris is my best friend, and together we have built a wonderful life. Andris has four children from a previous marriage. We share many meaningful moments together, creating memories with our eight children. We live in Fort Myers, Florida, where Andris is a building contractor and I handle renovation design.

Their Resilient Spirit

Tea is 17 and attends a local Christian school; her passions are cooking, nutrition, Krav Maga (a military self-defense and fighting system) and music. She is her own SHEro and has learned how to cope with several chronic health conditions that challenge her daily. She is extremely creative and compassionate. I am often in awe of her resilient spirit, incredible work ethic, and can-do attitude. Her future plans include becoming a chef and a functional nutrition practitioner.

My son Julian is now 26 and lives in a cottage on our property. Julian is compassionate, loving, and one of the smartest humans I know. As a young child, he struggled with learning differences and neurodiversity. After finding the right nutrition plan and school, Julian thrived. After graduating from high school, he went into the Army to become a medic. However, during some training exercises, he sustained injuries that ended his Army career. Julian is currently working part time and healing.

Hannah is married to a charismatic loving partner, Steven, and they have a precious little girl, Savannah. They live in West Palm Beach. Hannah is incredibly creative, passionate and full of life. She brings infectious energy and joy to all her projects. Hannah "lives out loud" and I aspire to be more like her.

Destin, my eldest, is happily married to a wonderful man, Ilich. He has a daughter, Olivia, and together, they are raising her in Bonita Springs, Florida. They live down the street from where my parents now live, and they are only a short drive from us. Destin has worked for a large health food store for many years in training and management. She is currently going to school to become a nurse practitioner and then a physician assistant. She also works part time at a local children's hospital in the emergency department.

Destin is an amazing human and everyone's go-to for good advice – or a kick in the pants. She is driven, and always balancing dozens of balls in the air while doing her absolute best at everything she tackles. She also shares and holds precious memories of our Sarina. Together, we keep her memory alive with stories and laughter.

My dad and Janet moved to the United States full time from England and are enjoying their best life. They live in Bonita

Springs and continue to be incredibly supportive and a loving force in our family.

Joy Is Within Us

I truly believe we create the life we live, and that everything moves us towards awareness and a deeper connection with our spirit within, each other, and the Divine. My wish for you is to recognize the divine order in your deepest valleys, and for you to experience the full expression of the wholeness of joy as we walk through this life together.

— EVONN PETERSON

Inspiration to Experience Joy

In life, we often focus on the verbs to do and to have, but *The SHEro Mindset* is about practicing the verb to BE. Use these affirmations to experience joy.

Be Grateful
Gratitude has the power to help us to shift from negative to positive emotions. A grateful heart is full of joy! The practice of gratitude can bring you into the present moment. Recognizing how others enhance your life with their gestures will bring you joy.

Be Perceptive
Life is a mosaic of experiences, and how we perceive them can change the outcome. When we are perceptive to what is really going on, we can develop more compassion and find forgiveness. We can grow from our experiences when we accept them as opportunities. This creates space for more joy.

Be Simple
Joy can be found in the simple moments – when we connect with like-minded people, or spend time with animals. Experiencing the simplicity of nature also brings joy.

Be Blissful
Focusing on and feeling our connection with others, with nature, and to the force of the universe, allows us to experience bliss. When we experience bliss, we are one with our source, with God. In this state, things flow smoothly and

we can create the life of our dreams. We can access Joy when we allow bliss into our lives.

Be Resilient

We are resilient when we face challenges and use our tools to move through them. Using the powers and tools that we have is how we become resilient. We can access Joy when we use our resilience to overcome challenges.

Joy Meditation

Joy is your friend

Joy is colorful, creative, and full of energy

It lives in you

This joy shows up in the most unexpected places

In moments when you least expect it

Joy has the power to remind us of the beauty of life

This power has the dust of fairies

and the playfulness of gnomes

It is the sound of angels and archangels singing us lullabies

This joy... brings us to the now,

to feel present and be a present

A true gift from God,

To witness life and its bliss!

One can be joyful, one can help others be joyful too

Joy makes you giggle and feel the warmest hugs.

Joy brings smiles and happiness

Joy is all it takes to bring us Hope

It is one of the secret ingredients of our resilience

Joy makes us fall in love, all over again

A heart full of joy is a heart of gold,

Let it be, let it be Joyful!

The Power of
LOVE

One day we will depart, and because of the Love we planted in each other's hearts, we will live on. Life is worthwhile when it is lived with Love. Love is not judgmental, not suffocating, not conditional. Love can heal, and Love can empower us to be our best selves.

*Love has many colors and flavors. It
transcends time, space, and even death.
Love is our heart's conviction propelling
us to act in difficult times. Love is the joy that
celebrates the beauty of life. Love is all.*

KAREN GUGGENHEIM

CHAPTER 4

Love

When I met Holly, I instantly felt a connection – almost like we knew each other from another life. I knew in the depth of my soul that Holly and I were not meeting casually. We shared a mission in life – even though, at the time, we did not know the magnitude of our mission. Our mission would change our lives forever.

Holly's journey in life has been very challenging. She always wanted to be a mother, and even though she had to confront many obstacles to achieve that dream, she knew her purpose in life was to have a lovely family.

Holly and I have become close friends; I was honored to share one of the most important moments of her life with her (the birth of her daughter). I am grateful we crossed paths in this life and that she calls me her sister. I call Holly my princess because she has all the qualities of one: persistence, gratitude, strength and a heart of gold.

Holly has an amazing capacity to love. She curates her life with kindness, and through her actions, she touches many people's hearts. Her eyes have the capacity to see far beyond the exterior to the heart of who someone is. Her hope is to inspire people to open their hearts and their lives with the virtue of Love.

Holly's tenacity, courage and persistence make her one of our SHEroes. In this chapter, she will share her story of love and kindness that has touched many lives.

— LULU

Love

Holly's Story
Devotion to Others

I was a carefree child with an adventurous soul. I grew up in a small town in northern Minnesota with a magnificent raging river running through the heart of it. It is an incredibly gorgeous part of the world, and I was fortunate to live there, although I did not know it at the time.

The Enchanted Forest

Our simple house was deep in the forest about five miles from town, and we had only a few neighbors. A lot of the time, I would walk alone between my house and town. On my walks, I loved picking berries and flowers, and exploring the forest. I walked freely in the woods, stopping to observe the complexity of nature. Sometimes I would lie down... I'd look up at the sky and admire the movement of the clouds.

I think I started to meditate when I was a child, but I didn't even know what I was doing. My mind was one with nature. I was so brave and did not fear the wildlife. I was fine with the moose, bears and deer around me. Sometimes I would even take a nap in the ferns. Can you imagine a child alone in the forest, just resting on the ground?

There was a bridge that crossed over the river that led into town. The raging rapids in the river were breathtaking and magnificent. The town was small, with no more than 500 people. My grandma Ruby had a café in town, and I spent time there. There was not a lot else going on in our small town. But

I was curious, so the forest was my playground. Even in the winter I spent a lot of time outdoors, playing with the snow and observing nature's magical beauty.

I am grateful for those times. My experiences as a child gave me the mindset I have today.

The Princess and the Castle

When I was 14, my parents divorced. I did not know they were having issues – it was sudden and unexplained for me – so I was shocked. My mom Judy and my father Terry had rarely argued or disagreed in front of me or my older brother, Adam.

Growing up as a teenager after the divorce was not always easy for me. There were dark moments and I experienced significant anxiety, although I did not actually realize what I was going through. I was angry with my parents for divorcing, but was not in touch with my emotions. I knew they loved me, but I was angry at them for breaking our family apart. If they could stop loving each other, then maybe they could stop loving me. My sense of security was gone; my castle had crumbled.

After my parents' split, my mom moved to a new city to pursue a college degree. I chose to stay with my father while finishing high school, but I was proud of my mother and missed her beyond words. I was still struggling with my emotions; anxiety became the center of my life. I felt unsafe, uncertain, and vulnerable as I tried to navigate what I was feeling. Family is everything to me and I felt I had lost mine.

Love

I was no longer the princess in the magical forest. I was an anxious teenager experiencing overwhelming emotions. I went from having carefree adventures and laughing a lot to being uncertain. My father remarried, and I did not know how to get along with my stepmom. I felt misunderstood and forgotten. It was a very difficult time for me.

The Village

During my senior year, my anger towards my parents blinded me and I needed something to change. My best friend Jodi was going through the same thing with her parents. Jodi understood my pain and we became even closer.

Jodi offered for me to move in with her and her father, Arden, for my last year of school. My parents agreed, because I was nearly 18. Jodi's house became my happy place. Being with my best friend made me feel loved and safe again – she was like a sister to me.

Arden became an important figure in my life. He was genuine and caring, and taught me lessons I needed to learn. It was like being in the darkness and finding a flashlight. Arden held the flashlight for me so I could see through my emotions. They gave me what I needed to move out of the darkness.

We Wanted It All

I have a brave spirit; after high school, I was ready for a change. So, in 1990 I packed everything up and moved away from the cold winters in Minnesota to sunny, warm Florida. I wanted to start a new life and leave some memories behind.

It was time to make new friends and start a career. After earning a bachelor's degree in legal studies in Florida, I considered going to law school.

In 2001, a few months before I was going to take the LSAT (law school entrance exam), I met my future husband Marc. We were introduced by a mutual friend at a holiday party. Neither of us was looking for anything serious, because we had both just ended relationships. When we first met, I was planning on leaving for law school. But, as the relationship grew, I was hesitant to leave because I knew that long-distance relationships are hard and rarely last. I decided to give us one year and see what would happen. Thank goodness I did, because we were meant to be. We became more serious as time went on, and eventually we moved in together. Marc proposed and we married in November 2004.

We were committed to each other, and wanted to build our family and raise our children with lots of Love. I was creating the perfect family and wanted to be the best mother in the world. We wanted to grow our businesses and have that picture-perfect family that you see on TV. We wanted it all!

The Perfect Storm

I have not shared this with many people, but it was a rough road to become a mother. I had five miscarriages before I gave birth to our first child, Nathan. It was emotionally exhausting to be pregnant and then lose the baby each time. Every time I became pregnant, we had so much hope, and then we would be heartbroken from losing our babies. When I finally did get pregnant with Nathan, I was considered high risk, because of the multiple prior miscarriages. And that pregnancy was not easy; I almost lost Nathan.

At that time in my life, I was afraid to use my voice, so I did what the doctors recommended and asked no questions. For Nathan's delivery, I was induced and had an epidural. It was not what I wanted at all, but I was nervous, so I went against my gut instincts. I believed the doctor who insisted that I could not give birth without an epidural.

After Nathan was born, I could not believe I was finally a mom. I was so overjoyed that our dream of a family had finally come true.

When Nathan was a baby, I was so judgmental of myself. I was also anxious and had no support system in place. When he was about 4 months old, I started taking him to "mommy and me" classes. I noticed that he was fussy and also not developing at the same rate as the other children. I was worried. Deep down inside, I knew something was not typical about his development. At times, I blamed myself – surely, I was doing something wrong, and it was my fault that he was not developing. I thought I sucked at being a mom, and searched for answers to try and solve the problems we were facing.

That feeling of joy about being a mother was still there, but in my gut, I knew something was off. He was my first child, so I had no other children to compare him to, but I still had a deep sense that something was wrong. I just didn't know what it was, and did not have the tools yet to accept it.

The hardest part for me was Nathan's constant crying. I would try to soothe him, but he was screaming almost nonstop and it was torture. All I wanted to do was comfort him, but I had no support around me. He would only fall asleep for 20 minutes at a time and then wake up again screaming. I discovered this crazy "shush, rock, pat" routine that took about 20 solid minutes to get him to sleep – and I had to be standing up, or it did not work. Once he fell asleep in my arms, I would lay him down and he would sleep for 20 minutes, but then he would wake up screaming and the vicious cycle would start over again.

I prayed for all that to end, but it went on and on. He did not sleep through the night until he was about 5 years old. Sleep deprivation was the hardest thing I have had to live through. It was a very lonely and isolating time for me. I had wanted to live the ideal family life, but I felt I was failing. I did not trust my instincts and was unsure of myself.

I was so sleep-deprived that I had suicidal thoughts. If sleep deprivation was not enough, Nathan struggled with feeding and my postpartum depression was magnified. Imagine being a mother and not being able to feed your child. His feeding issues were so bad, and his weight was so low, that the doctor considered placing a feeding tube in Nathan. I was exhausted, but I was not going to give up. I loved him way too much.

I worried that others would think I was a failure as a mom. I gave myself no grace or compassion. I was nervous that I was doing something wrong, and that all of this was my fault. I had a distorted definition of what being a good mom was. Being a first-time mother, I had nothing from my past to go on, to guide me. Why doesn't parenting come with a manual? I did not feel like I had the answers.

But maybe I did?

My love for Nathan and my family, and knowing he needed me to survive, was what got me through the darkest time of my life.

The Thanksgiving Nightmare

Marc and I still really wanted to expand our family. I became pregnant again in 2008 around Thanksgiving. Nathan was not even 2 yet. We were at Marc's parents' home, and I started having severe abdominal pain. I called my doctor, but he dismissed my concerns and said he would see me the next day. The pain was so brutal that I was soon lying on the bathroom floor in severe agony. No one anticipated the nightmare that was about to happen.

Because the doctor had dismissed my pain, I thought that it was all in my head. When I saw the doctor the next day (the same one who delivered Nathan and had convinced me I could not give birth without an epidural), he said that – given my history – I was probably having another miscarriage. Or possibly, it was endometriosis (which occurs when tissue that originates from the lining of the uterus starts growing outside it).

The doctor said, "We just need to wait and see, but you are probably losing the baby. Only time will tell."

Little did he know that I was suffering from a life-threatening ectopic pregnancy that was about to burst. The doctor failed me when he did not pay attention to the level of pain I was experiencing. For the next two weeks, I went about my life in severe pain, thinking, *I must follow my doctor's instructions.* I did not trust my own instincts.

Two weeks later, my ectopic pregnancy ruptured in the middle of the night. I could feel life slipping away from me as I laid on the bathroom floor again. I had internal bleeding and was rushed to the hospital for an emergency surgery.

When the emergency room doctor explained what was happening, she told me that my doctor (the one who had failed me) was on the way to perform the surgery. I was beyond terrified that I was not going to make it through the surgery. I had absolutely no trust in him at that point.

Angels on Earth

One of the things that I believe saved me in that situation was that the anesthesiologist on call was Karl, a dear friend's husband. He was an angel, and it was a miracle. He reassured me that he would not leave my side. I know that I would not have made it out of surgery if he hadn't been there looking out

Love

for me. I had lost over 50 percent of my blood. I almost died a few times during the surgery.

After that experience, my anxiety level went through the roof. I had almost lost my life. My son was not eating at all, and still was not sleeping well. My mother came for visits, but she lived far away at that time. I felt lonely and had little support. A few months later, we had more terrible news – my husband, Marc, was diagnosed with late onset juvenile diabetes. I was afraid we were going to lose him. Those were very difficult times for our family.

Not long after that, we were invited to a birthday party at House of Gaia. Marc's hobby is playing drums in a band, and one of the band members was throwing a party for his son there. Nathan was around the same age as the birthday boy, so we were guests, and that was when I met Lulu, the studio's owner. From the moment I arrived, I felt something special. Lulu and I connected deeply and we became best friends quickly.

I knew I could trust Lulu, so I started to open up to her. I asked her for help. I started taking Nathan to her art studio, and she and I just observed him. He did not want to spend time inside; he looked for the door and wanted to escape. She would open the door and we would follow him into the parking lot while he was running. He would climb the stairs; he would go anywhere if we let him. At the time, he would not look at us or stop if we called his name. She invited each member of our family to spend time with him and her at the studio.

Lulu wanted to find the right way to tell me about her concerns regarding Nathan's development. One afternoon, she invited me to go to see a documentary at a local cinema in Fort Myers, about 40 minutes from Naples. I brought a pizza, and she brought her mom. That was the first time I met Lislane (Lulu's mom). I was excited to spend time with them, but did not fully understand why she wanted me to see the documentary.

The film was about children who have difficulty developing, and about parents who experienced what I had with Nathan. These were children with autism. I was nervous and my heart was pounding rapidly. My intuition screamed loud and clear... I have a son with autism. The simple truth of that homemade documentary resonated with me.

When the documentary ended, we stood and started walking to the car. It was at that moment that I knew the truth; I collapsed right there. Lulu and her mom picked me up from the floor, but I could not breathe – I was drowning in my tears. It was like a thousand glasses had shattered inside of my heart.

At that moment, my reality changed. I was going to need to fight for him like I had never fought before. At the time – 15 years ago – there was not much awareness about autism. My child suffered, cried a lot, and struggled to survive. So, I knew

Love

I had to become my own SHEro in order to advocate for my son.

Finding My Voice

I felt like I was going mad. Our family was experiencing a lot of medical challenges. It took us a while to find doctors who were supportive. The truth is that doctors are human, and they don't have all the answers or a crystal ball. I learned that we have the right to advocate for ourselves and our loved ones by asking questions. A good doctor will say that they don't have all the answers. It is OK to get a second opinion and keep looking until you find the answers you need.

During the whole process of seeking quality medical care for my family, something special happened: I found my voice! I learned how to be an excellent advocate for myself, and for my family. Our challenges taught me to speak up, and this has been HUGE for me.

During the first two years of Nathan's life, when I was seeking answers, most everyone said, "Don't worry, he will grow out of it." But deep inside, I sensed he needed me to search for more answers. I was in denial, so I was happy each time someone told me not to worry. But I knew. As he grew, it became more apparent that something was different about him, but I was not ready for the truth yet.

Confronting the Truth

When Nathan was 2, we found a neurologist who could see right through me. I remember the day he sat me down in his office, grabbed my face, looked me straight in the eye, and said, "Your son has autism. I don't know what things will be like for him or you. No one does," He went on to say, "You can let it break you or make you!"

At that moment, I knew I was meant to be Nathan's mom. I am here for a reason, and he needed me to stand up for this fight. So that is exactly what I did. I stood up and have not sat down since then. In order to advocate for Nathan, I had to find my voice. The most ironic part of this whole journey is that my voice began to grow because my son has non-verbal autism. To this day, words still do not come out of his mouth, but I have learned that there is so much more to communication than words.

Nathan is 15 now, and I have fully accepted his diagnosis. I have moments where I project doom and gloom into the future, but then I bring myself back to the present moment and remember that he is a very happy boy. Nathan is joyful and has an amazing personality that shines. He has likes and dislikes just like any of us, and he experiences the full rainbow of human emotions. Nathan's life is filled with love, and I am lucky to be his mom!

Love Is My Compass

Our family is all about love and acceptance, and we did not let Nathan's diagnosis, Marc's diagnosis, or my diagnosis stop us. It was important to us to keep on growing our family and expanding our love. After my 10th miscarriage, we considered adoption, but decided to try in vitro fertilization (IVF) first. It was going to be very hard on my body, so I agreed with Marc to do just one round.

We consulted with a doctor, and she felt that we were good candidates for IVF. She was able to pinpoint what was happening with my body and had a likely solution to prevent miscarriage. All I needed to do was to follow her guidance with hormone injections, a medicine routine, and infusions at the time that the embryos would be transferred. It sounded simple enough, and we signed up right away.

Several doctors told us that if I followed the recommendations, I would have a really good chance of having a healthy baby. We felt hopeful that we were about to experience a true miracle.

Stairway to Heaven
Finally, I thought, *The pregnancy will happen and soon I might be a mom for the second time.* How is this for serendipity: the names of the head nurse and my doctor were the same as mine!! Holly, which kind of sounds like "holy." The trifecta! Everything was aligning.

During that time, my days were filled with treatments and tests. We also had to decide what to do with the extra embryos. Waiting for the peak moment made for weeks of incredible intensity. I felt good and was confident, but I was tested in every area of life: spiritual, physical, and emotional. In addition, we were still sorting out the best treatments for

Nathan. We took him to several doctors, feeding therapy, occupational therapy, speech therapy, and to clinics all over the country – as I continued to improve my skills in navigating his care.

During the IVF process, a friend asked if I wanted to risk my life to have another retarded child. I could not believe she would say that. Her question rocked me a little bit, but I didn't let it stop us. I put aside her judgment of me, walked away from that relationship, and honored our choice. We were committed to love and wanted to grow our family. We focused on living in the moment.

The Countdown

Marc and I were confident about our decision, and so we moved forward with the IVF treatment. There was a 10 percent chance of an anaphylactic reaction during the infusion, but I trusted my doctor and she felt that it was going to be fine. I trusted my gut and I had a positive mindset. I believe that every one of us is at risk every day for various reasons; I chose to overlook that fear.

In IVF, we could end up with many embryos or none. While we were waiting for the time of infusion, the number of viable embryos declined from 20 in the first few days to nine, to four, and then to two. Finally, there was just one embryo on the night before the implant transfer.

Everything was perfectly aligned chemically. They kept checking me for that perfect moment – and then I got a

Love

last-minute call from my doctor, who told me something unexpected.

The Moment of Suspense

The call came at around 4:30 p.m. the day before I was supposed to get up at 6 a.m. and drive from Naples to Miami to have the transplant of our one miracle embryo. After months of intense preparation, I was ready. We were praying that the transplant would be the answer to our prayers to complete our family.

But my doctor began to tell me that the owner of the clinic had decided that I was too high a risk to have the needed infusion treatment.

I was ready and my body was ready. This was the 11th hour! I asked, "What are you talking about?"

She said, "Well, I ran one other test on you that just came back. All along, I thought the results would be good, but you are at a higher risk than I expected. It is a new treatment, and my boss feels that we can't afford the risk."

I asked, "What is the increased risk?"

She said, "For anyone else, it is 10 percent, but you are at 20 percent risk of a reaction."

I said that I would take that risk. She agreed with me, but said that her hands were tied. They were willing to give us our money back – or do the transfer of the embryo without the infusion. However, she knew that would likely end in another miscarriage. Another option they offered was to freeze the embryo and see if another doctor would be willing to take the risk. But the embryo would likely not freeze well, so that was not a good option.

It was a beyond-against-the-odds moment. My body was at the peak time for the embryo transfer to happen. I had been receiving multiple hormones and many medications to prepare my body for that moment. Everything was lined up perfectly, so it was now or never.

Rollercoaster of Emotions

For months, we were going through the whole process. Marc and I had so many hopes, and we felt that it was our last chance. This news was the worst-case scenario.

During the weeks leading up to this day, when they were giving us daily updates about the embryos growing, I felt a sense of life. Those were our babies! It was emotional and we were now down to one viable embryo that could not be frozen. The embryo would not have the chance to survive without the implant, and now they were not willing to give me the infusion of immunoglobulin that I needed to stop my body from attacking the pregnancy.

The worst part was when my doctor told us she could give us our money back. I could not have cared any less about the money. This was the possibility of life we were talking about.

My SHEro mindset kicked in; I took three deep breaths and went into immediate action. I guessed that I had about 30 minutes to come up with a plan to save our embryo. I can't tell you if I was breathing or even speaking at that point. The irony was that Nathan was in with his speech therapist and I was in the waiting room when I received the call.

I called a doctor who I trusted; I knew he would be willing to help if I could reach him. As I called, repeatedly, I thought about the infusion medication, immunoglobulin. This is no ordinary medicine. It has to be preordered from a specialty pharmacy and kept in climate-controlled conditions. It is very expensive, and if I was lucky enough to reach the doctor, would he be lucky enough to have the medication delivered in time? The embryo needed to be transferred in only a few short hours, or my body would not be receptive if I did not get that infusion. We were aiming at a bull's-eye, with only one arrow, from 100 miles away.

A Miracle

After 20 minutes and about 150 power dials resulting in automated messages, I finally hit enough buttons that a human answered. I don't think I was making any sense on the phone, but the nurse who answered said that she would catch the doctor before he left for the day.

She put me on hold, and it felt like time was in slow motion. When the doctor picked up the phone, he immediately shouted, "I will do it." He said, "Get the embryo transfer in a few hours and then come to me. I have to hang up so I can get the medicine in time." We had only a few words; it was minutes before 5 p.m.

By grace, he was able to reach one of his contacts and get the special infusion ordered in time. He said, "I will give you the infusion personally and stay with you in case you have a reaction. Just get the embryo transfer and come to me."

I felt like I was underwater while he was talking to me, because my ears were ringing and everything seemed muffled. When I called Marc and told him what was happening, he was pretty upset. We decided to hire a driver to take us because we needed to drive three hours to Miami for the embryo transfer, and then immediately drive to Daytona, another two hours away, where the doctor would be waiting. He would give me an eight-hour infusion of the medication to keep my body from attacking the embryo.

From that moment on, it was like I was floating. I was calm and meditative, just like my times in the woods. I had a deep sense that everything was meant to be.

We went through the entire procedure, and the doctor said jokingly, "Now go home and don't move." Then he became serious, and said, "This is going to work." I felt it myself.

Sure enough, only a few days later, I had a positive pregnancy test. It was a true miracle in so many ways.

Love

In 2022, our daughter, Ariana, will be 11 years old. Marc and I are so proud of who she is as a person.

Ariana is one of the most compassionate children I know. She is an excellent sister and a very caring friend. Her kindness and care teach me every day how to be kinder, and how to love myself and others in ways that I never imagined. I am constantly reflecting on the words she expresses or her simple acts of kindness. Nathan and Ariana became my best teachers.

I can't wait for Ariana to grow enough to grasp the intensity of her beginning. She was meant to be born into this world for a larger reason than just to grow our family. Ariana inspires others to be kind. Real love needs kindness to thrive.

Here is what Lulu would like to share about Ariana: "I was invited by Holly and Marc to be with them in the hospital during their baby girl's delivery. I was the first person (other than the hospital staff) to see Ariana. Her birth was so powerful and yet peaceful. I witnessed a leader being born. Ariana and I have similar stories – both of us have parents who went through a lot to bring us into the world. I am so proud to be a part of her family; it has been my honor to have mentored Ariana since she was a toddler. She leads from her heart, and I can't wait to see what kind of SHEro she will become. I believe she will have a positive impact on this world. Bravo, Ariana! Lulu loves you so much, and you can always count on me."

Rise Up Stronger

Here is what I have learned through my journey: when things seem hopeless, get up and try again. We rise up stronger each time we move through a challenge. Our challenges can help us to grow stronger and we can learn how to be grateful for each precious moment, whether it is big or small. Every moment can lead us to more love, kindness and Joy!

I believe that each part of my life journey has happened for a reason and I live with **love** and pure gratitude. Being grateful feels beautiful. Love and gratitude have given me the grace and strength to bear the news of serious diagnoses for both my children called CVID (common variable immune deficiency). CVID, a type of primary immune deficiency (PID), has also triggered their bodies to develop rare, complicated autoimmune conditions. Also, Nathan has recently developed stage 2 chronic kidney disease. All of this means that their immune systems do not work normally, so they need to have weekly infusions of antibodies to fight things off.

When I meet someone new and I talk about our family's medical challenges, it could seem heavy at first. Many people are shocked and ask me how I do it (especially during the pandemic). I say that it is all how you look at it. I feel like my life is full, and my children are happy, and our family has a beautiful life. Marc and I could live like they are already dying or gone, or we can live in the moment. There is no "perfect" for anyone, because none of us know what can happen. I choose to teach my children to live in the moment, and that feels amazing.

I am truly grateful for Marc, Nathan, Ariana, my extended family, my friends and my childhood hometown. Those childhood experiences of freedom and independence in the forest, when I was on my own with nature, have sustained me through the hard times. I feel that my deep connection to nature very early on in life taught me to be present and to breathe, and that has made a difference in my life.

With time and wisdom, I was able to understand why my parents divorced, and now I have had a beautiful, harmonious relationship with both of my parents. I am grateful for both of my parents. Because of their love for me, I am a loving parent. As parents, we will not be perfect; our job is to be loving. I am grateful for their love, and that passes on through me to my children.

After all that I have experienced, I have the deepest compassion and empathy for all humans, because every one of us has a story. We all experience the rainbow of emotions, and that is what connects us. Love is my compass and it guides me through everything. Love is acceptance; Love makes us brave.

— HOLLY SHAPIRO

Inspiration to Embody Love

In life, we often focus on the verbs to do and to have, but *The SHEro Mindset* is about practicing the verb to BE. Use these suggestions to embody love.

Be Open

Being open to diversity is the first tool of love. Accepting means that you respect the differences in others. When you are open to fully accepting yourself, you can accept others. By accepting and letting go of the control, you can release your fears to find love. Be open to accepting what is.

Be Giving

Love is the answer to many questions. When we give love without conditions, we can free ourselves to receive love. Give love without the fear of rejection, and without the need of recognition. Love given can be the remedy to all ills.

Be Forgiving

Forgiving means to love yourself and to move forward with your life, despite others' mistakes. It is the ultimate test of who you are. Forgive yourself first, so that you can have love in your heart to forgive others. You don't need to forget; you just need to keep loving yourself.

Be Compassionate

How can we understand compassion on a deep level? We want to understand others' perspectives, but not feel their pain.

Showing compassion is to be present and to hold a loving space for someone in need – without judgment or advice.

Be Active

Love can be a verb. Pure love is to give to others what they need and want. It is also acting selflessly and with kindness. When you are in the space of love, everything seems possible. Love with care, love with respect, knowing that everything and everyone is worthy. Act with Love.

Love Meditation

Love... can be the remedy for all sorrows
Love... can heal your deep wounds
Love... is the nutrient for all souls
Love... can ignite your spirit
Love... is the reason to be alive
Love... can connect you to your purpose
Love... is the key to happiness
Love... can bring you joy
Love... is a thing worth striving for
Love... is the force behind everything you do
Love is powerful, Love is needed, Love can be your acts
So... Embody Love, Live Love, Be Love
Love yourself, love nature, love your environment
Love others... simply love
Love, love, love, love... is transformative
Love is the answer to all questions

The Power of
COURAGE

Let courage ignite our souls. Let it be the energy that helps us make decisions and take action. Let it be the power of all powers, the fuel that moves us in the direction of the brightest light. Let courage burn in the center of our core, as Mother Nature's courage burns in her core. Let it heal from that core and let it be all part of transformation, rebirth and unconditional love.

*Courage is the choice to confront
pain, danger, uncertainty or intimidation.
The virtue of courage moves us,
pushing it forward in life anyway,
as our wisdom leads us
to do what is right despite our fears.*

REBECCA WALTERS

CHAPTER 5

Courage

In 2009, when Suzy was searching for a creative outlet for her youngest children, Maxim and Elizabeth, she found the programs at House of Gaia. I will never forget the first time I saw Suzy's big, beautiful, green eyes as she walked through our studio's doors. They were so vibrant and full of zest. Suzy and I are both talkative, friendly and spontaneous. She told me all about her love of travel – especially to Paris, Greece, and Sicily – and we found a shared passion.

Suzy also shared with me that she had lost her oldest son, leaving her family to grieve terribly. I was honored to create an art program to help Maxim and Elizabeth heal. I believe art is such a powerful tool to facilitate one's expressiveness and to move through life's experiences. The classes at my studio with Maxim and Elizabeth were interactive, creative, and serene, and I felt connected to them as I developed respect for what they were going through.

By 2011, we had moved from being an art studio to being a nonprofit center. Suzy and her family participated in a group offered by Compassionate Friends called Rainbow, designed for children who had lost their siblings.

The SHEro Mindset

Suzy has endured difficult challenges and heartbreaking losses, but she is compassionate, loving, and fun. She is a SHEro. In this chapter, Suzy opens her heart and tells us her story. Two years ago, it would not have been possible for Suzy to share her experiences, as she still had so much to process and heal. Now she feels the moment has arrived, and she is ready.

— LULU

Suzy's Story
The Connections Beyond Life

The process of telling the following story was a bit daunting, but Lulu made it easy with her compassion and love. Meeting the other SHEroes was an amazing experience. With these heroic women, I felt accepted and appreciated. I felt that I fit in with them, in a world where I sometimes do not feel that way.

Open Heart

My story has elements of despair and tragic losses, but most of all, it is a story of love and courage. It is about my spiritual journey to find serenity, peace and joy. It is about my lessons, my dreams and my traumas. Also, it includes an immense amount of healing, self-discovery and self-development. I had to endure so much to preserve myself. As my family and I are still confronting challenges, I keep finding the courage in my heart to continue on a path of balance and mental health.

I am telling my story to reach as many people as possible and to connect with your heart. I know that my story can help those who are suffering from loss, or are experiencing anxiety or conflict. I want you to know: you are not alone.

There is hope – and endless opportunities for healing – if you have courage. Stay focused on your heart, and never give up on your dreams. The good news is that you are also going to have moments of happiness that can be achieved with patience, time and compassion. Breathe each time you experience fear. Rebirth yourself as many times as needed to keep moving forward. You are more than your story – you are a loving spirit, experiencing a full life.

My Galaxy

I was born and raised in St. Louis, Missouri. I was a happy child who had everything a child needed in her life. My father Vincent was Sicilian, and my mother Nadine was a saint – a gem, very loving and caring. I am the combination of both. I have strong genes from my dad – I can be emotional and I am easily triggered. But I can also be kind and gentle like my mother.

My parents owned a bridal business, and I spent a lot of time at our factory socializing with the employees. They became my family too! I loved to dress up in discarded dresses. Later, in my teens, I became a runway model for the company, which I enjoyed very much.

I was raised mostly as an only child; I am the baby of the family. My sister Rosalyn (Roz) is 11 years older than I am, and my brother Vincent is 14 years older. I remember not having many children to play with as a child, and that motivated me to have a large family.

Most of my time in my teenage years was spent with my soulmate Scott. We met in 1976 at the local bowling alley, playing pinball and foosball games. We were 13 and 15. If anyone believes in love at first sight, that would be me. Scott was tall, handsome and smart. I guess it was just meant to be.

In college, I moved to Denver, Colorado to pursue musical theater and study the French language. Scott followed me to Denver – we were inseparable, and life was good.

In 1989, we married in St. Louis, Missouri at Holy Redeemer Catholic Church. I was 25 and he was 27. Our wedding was the grandest of all! It was a dreamy, Italian, over-the-top wedding. We had 500 guests at a fabulous sit-down dinner, with beautiful flowers and wonderful music. My dress was gorgeous – it was designed by my mother, who was a pattern maker and designer. The beautiful white lace was from New York and Italy. I will never forget that magical night – it is always in my heart.

I became pregnant on our two-week honeymoon and stayed that way for the next eight years. We were blessed with five beautiful children, all very close in age. I realized my dream of a large family. Life was difficult and busy, yet blissful.

The Stars

To understand the complexity of my galaxy, you need to know us! Our family has a great sense of humor. We are emotive, sensitive and close. Having a big family can be the most exciting thing in the world, or it can be a constant struggle. In our house, we love a lot – sometimes too much!

As the mother of this family, I am constantly worrying about the health, welfare and safety of my children and husband. I treat them as if they have lost contact with their own needs, desires and sense of self. I feel responsible for everything and everyone's behavior. There is always a feeling of push and pull – we want to be together, and then we don't. What we feel for each other is intense, and there are so many emotions with us. In my family, we love like crazy – to the point of losing perspective, patience and respect for each other.

Scott is a natural musician, a great guitar player who performed in the St. Louis area. He passed his talent onto our children, who picked up a lot from their father.

Our oldest son, Nicholas, was a smart, happy, kind child who wanted to make everyone smile. He taught me patience and kindness; and maybe, I taught him the same. We always learned from each other. Nick grew to be tall and strong, and had a great talent for music. He started playing the cello at 4 years old, and also played the violin and the guitar. Nick was our rock star.

Our second son, Tyler, was handsome, tall and humble. He also was musically gifted and played the guitar. He loved to play and write songs for me. I called him my shining star. We loved skiing together. Tyler was never afraid of doing tricks or skiing in the woods with me. He was sweet-natured, but also needed the thrill of excitement.

Nick and Tyler had a very close relationship. From a very young age, Nick protected and loved his younger brother. He became Tyler's voice, because Tyler refused to speak until he was 3 years old. Later on, Nick became Tyler's mentor.

Our third child, Tony, had the most beautiful blue eyes and chubby cheeks. He was giant, charismatic and liked playing football. Everyone loved Tony! He may have been the biggest child on the block, but he was also the most popular – he made friends easily. I called him my superstar, because he was such a Superman fan.

After three boys, we had our girl! Can you imagine – finally, a girl? We named her Elizabeth after the queen of England. And she is nothing but a queen! I knew in my heart she would be my strongest. She is also very artistic and loves to draw. She has always been a hard worker; our warrior.

Then there is our baby, Maxim. We call him Max. He grew up to be an artistic philosopher. You cannot be around Max without having a deep conversation. He always has a bright smile on his face; his love for his family shows. His good looks and contagious laughter make it hard not to engage with him.

Our family's path has been full of scenic turns and scary cliffs. What my husband and I didn't know was how much our children would suffer from the curse of drug addiction. Tragically, our family story turned out to be one centered around addiction and codependency. Those factors have affected our ability to have peaceful and healthy relationships.

Nick the Rockstar

By 2008 we were living in Florida, and little by little, things started to fall apart. I was raising the children and taking care of my parents. Life was filled with a spectrum of emotions and expectations. I was no longer the carefree girl in the wedding dress factory. Nick, our oldest, was only 17 years old, but wanted to declare independence from us.

"Mom, I graduated from high school and have a good job at a coffee shop. There's this apartment and these guys, and they want me to move in – I can afford it." My Nick was ready to become a man and start his own life. So he moved out of our house and stayed with his friends. He was living his life.

One day, I stopped by to say hi to Nick at work. That was the last time I would see him alive. His last words to me were shouted so everyone could hear: "I love you, Ma."

Not long after that visit at his workplace, my phone rang, and it was the police calling me to tell me that my son was dead. Nick did not do many drugs – but it only took a couple of pills to kill him while he was sleeping.

Everything immediately went dark.

I could not even breathe.

I lost myself completely.

I could not get out of bed.

My body was heavy, and poisoned by negative emotions.

It was hard to open my eyes.

I only knew how to cry; how to sob.

I couldn't take care of my other children or my parents.

I couldn't take care of myself.

Courage

The cemetery was the only place I wanted to go. I felt exhausted. I would visit Nick's grave and just lie there, rolling on the grass. I could barely move. I cried, laid there, and cried some more. I felt like I was disappearing with each day that passed.

While there was a lot of sadness and a lot of madness, sometimes a ray of light appeared, seemingly out of nowhere. Something small, but powerful and transformative, penetrated through the sorrow, the pain, and the agony. It was like a laser light that pointed to a brighter future. Was this light an angel, a feeling of hope? Or was it my heart, signaling me that I had to go on?

One day I was at the cemetery, I heard a ring. I looked down at my old flip phone, opened it, and read the screen: "Download Guitar Tuner Now." OK, I don't know anything about guitars; I was confused, surprised and stunned. I thought, Why is this happening? What is going on? Even if I had the smartphone of today, I wouldn't be able to download something. I asked, "What is going on with this phone?"

Silence...

I looked up...

I saw rainbows in the sky. I was in awe. They were so colorful, so harmonious, and so strong. Slowly, I stopped crying and rolling in the grass. This was the first time I sensed Nick's presence since his death – it was just like old times when he spent time with me. Nick was alive – he was right there with me, telling me to stop crying. I could feel him saying to me, "I'm here, you know... I'm here, Mom. It's OK. I'm here right now. Your Nick." I heard his message loud and clear from heaven.

When everything is sad, the mind looks for little miracles to happen. They remind us that the ones we love are not gone completely; they are here, somewhere among us. This spiritual experience happened before the first anniversary of Nick's death. I am so grateful I can still feel his presence. This is the power of love – never underestimate this power. It is something unique. It keeps our mind, body and soul connected – helping us to survive, giving us hope.

The Island of Nicholas

I needed that hope. We all did. Losing Nick dramatically changed the landscape of our family. None of us felt right after that – his brothers and his sister missed him terribly. Scott suffered so much, too; it was hard to watch him trying to survive his grief.

Time continued to pass. In 2009, as we approached the first anniversary of Nick's death, I was just learning how to survive. Normally, the anticipation of such a first anniversary would be terrifying for most families. In grieving programs, I've seen hundreds of parents anticipate the one-year anniversary of a death with lots of angst. It feels like the entire world is going to collapse and blow up. Waiting was too much to bear; so,

I decided to take a trip with my daughter Elizabeth – to run away from the sadness.

We went to Europe for a month, visiting cousins in Sicily and my best girlfriend in Switzerland. We also went to Rome and visited Paris, my second home. We were everywhere. We took a cruise to the Greek islands, and one morning, we stopped on the island of Santorini. It was exactly one year since Nick's death, and I had forgotten.

That day I saw Nicholas's name everywhere. All the shops and restaurants were dedicated to Saint Nicholas. It was amazing to experience another encounter with Nick. Just like that, he was telling me: "Ma, I am here. I'm here. I'm here." And I could not stop smiling.

On that day in Santorini, I was soothed, even though I was still grieving. I felt my son's spirit again and my heart sang. I was so grateful, because I could have been in many other places on earth, but there I was on the island of Santorini, Saint Irene. For me, it was the "island of Nicholas" as I felt the presence of my son. I don't believe in coincidences, but rather in fate, and that our stories are written even before we have lived them. This experience, on the anniversary of Nick's death, confirmed my belief in destiny.

Only a few years later, reality struck again. Time did not help us to heal. Instead, it brought us more grief. I was learning how complex my galaxy was, and just how much courage I possessed.

Tyler the Shining Star

This is Tyler's love story. Tyler and Madison had been together since they were in their early teens – just like Scott and I had been. I knew they were too young for marriage, but just like Romeo and Juliet, theirs was a story full of passion, love and struggles.

Madison became pregnant, and they had a beautiful baby boy. They were so young – Tyler was 20 and she was just 19. They decided to get married.

Tyler and Madison lived together and were planning their wedding. I was happily helping them put the ceremony together. But they were young, and confused about their own identities. Sometimes they were in love, and sometimes they weren't in love. They did not know how to separate who was who – they were codependent and constantly fighting. They loved each other like crazy.

A few months before their wedding, they had a change of heart. Tyler was not ready to commit to his fiancée. It looked like, despite having a baby, they were not going to be together. Tyler was depressed, and had been taking pills. The situation with Madison led him to increase the number of pills he was taking. He was lost – Madison had been the love of his life, and he could not bear being separated from his baby boy. He was very confused.

Scott and I attended a family reunion in St. Louis, and when we returned, we went over to Tyler and Madison's house.

Courage

We wanted to help Tyler sort out his situation, but we had not known how serious his depression was, or just how much help he needed. As we arrived, I felt in my heart and soul that something was wrong.

Scott found Tyler unconscious, and told me to call 911; he was desperately trying to bring Tyler back to life. I did not want to go inside of Tyler's room, and only partially saw his body. My heart stopped. When the paramedics arrived, It was already too late. He was gone.

My mind was spinning. *Why did this happen? Why didn't we arrive in time? Why is this happening again?* I can't tell you; I don't know how to describe what it is like to lose a second child. A deep, deep darkness descended upon me. Tyler's funeral was surreal. How did I find the strength to write his eulogy? Everything was so chaotic.

Madison had been planning to marry Tyler and now he was gone. They were supposed to be a happy family; instead, she was saying goodbye to the father of her baby. Tyler was gone, and the wedding would never happen. Tyler's death was too much for Madison, and within two months, she was gone too. Our dear Madison, so full of life and dreams, was gone. We had loved her like a daughter and were devastated. There are no words to express what it was like.

Their baby boy, our grandson, was just 8 months old. Tyler and Madison left behind an amazing child who has the best parts of each of his parents. I see Tyler when I look at him.

He's growing up so fast, but in a safe bubble, full of love and family. He is our pride and joy; he is so creative, just like his dad. He plays the piano and composes his own music – truly special. He loves soccer. He is our little miracle child, our blessing. I know that Tyler and Madison are here in spirit, protecting him and loving him.

Questions for God

I was a good Catholic woman; I was raised to do the right things in life. I taught French in a Catholic school. My life was supposed to be happy; I am an authentically happy person. So I questioned God: "If I was so good, why did I have to suffer?" For many years, I felt betrayed by God; I was angry at God. How could a loving God take my children from me? There were a lot of questions – and few answers.

Awful things can happen to good people, like us. But it is hard to understand a life with so much sorrow and pain. How can I have it all, and then lose so much? How can one person cope with so many losses?

The voices inside of my head back then were cold and ugly – like a horror movie with an awful soundtrack. They were telling me:

It happened again.

It's going to happen again.

It's happening again.

This isn't going to work out.

Why would it work out?

Bad things are going to happen.

Maybe I am cursed.

I caused all these things.

I had to remind myself, Breathe. I had to tell the voices to STOP. I asked, *What am I supposed to learn? How can I find acceptance?*

You may wonder if God answered my questions. The answer is, no. But I will find the answers as I learn the lessons. We are here on this earth to experience everything.

The Aftermath

One of the tragic things that happened when I lost my children is that I also lost close, long-term friends. My tragic, chaotic life was too much for them to witness. I had known my friend, who lives in Switzerland, since the fourth grade. We grew up together and made many memories. She was so supportive, like a sister. During the darkest time of my life, she moved back to the United States to help me. She cared for my parents when I couldn't take care of myself after Tyler died.

Today, she doesn't talk to me anymore. I know I was a mess, and she could not handle my mess. No one could. Even though she just wanted to help me – to be connected to me, to show her love – in the end, she could not. She could not relate to my pain or see me suffering so much. It was too much for her. I love her and I am so grateful for all the years we shared. My hope is that one day, I will have a chance to give her back some of what she gave to my family and me.

People came to be afraid of my curse. Everything in the dark seems so wrong, and is too much for most people. I would run into people that I knew, or they would see me out of the corner of their eye, and they would literally go the other way. They didn't know what to say to me.

I've heard that one loses about 90 percent of their friends – good friends – after one loses a child. In my case, it was true. And those losses made me feel that I had lost my place in the world.

Desert Roses

After the losses of two of my children – three, if you count Madison – I felt totally broken, lost and mad. I had failed as a parent. I felt intimidated by my friends; I felt judged as a person. Wherever I went, it felt like I had a mark on me – like I was being criticized for the tragic events in my life. I needed to escape from Florida. And my remaining children desperately needed me to protect them – to take them away from the drama, from our tragic past. It was time to create a new life, a new me. We needed a new start.

I chose the Arizona desert, to be away from everything and everyone who knew me. I thought, Maybe in the desert, things would be different. I had a lot of hope; I wanted things to change. We all needed to heal. I had separated from Scott; I was desperately trying to rewrite my story.

My parents were aging and my mom was very ill. Mom was smart, loving and caring. She was my best friend! Despite her fragility, she gave me her blessing to move to Arizona and leave Florida.

Sadly, my mother died the day I moved into my "mountain home." On June 3, 2016, at the age of 88, my mom graduated to heaven. The gate to my front door was covered with roses in full bloom, and a giant rainbow was encircling them.

I am grateful that Mom and I emptied our souls together before she died, so I was at peace knowing that everything had been said and done. My mom and I had closure.

I am also grateful that my friend Helen was with me in Arizona. She never judged me, so I felt comfortable around her. I knew I could talk to her about anything, and vice versa. I feel so privileged to still have her in my life. She is a strong woman and still my angel. I needed a friend so badly, and she gave me strength to find my courage.

A Cry for Help

My son Tony and I decided to travel back to Florida to bury my mom. On the first day we were in Naples, he went out to get drugs and a new tattoo. When Tony came back to my mom's house, he locked himself in the bathroom. He was in there for hours.

The SHEro Mindset

I was out running errands, preparing for my mother's funeral; getting her dress, her pearls. I came back to the house and looked for Tony. There was no sign of him. I went straight to the bathroom and kicked the door down – he was slumped against the wall, passed out. Oh my God!

I did not have any Narcan. Tony was rushed to the hospital. My son was battling for his life while I was at the funeral home saying farewell to my mother. It was insanity; I really didn't understand what was happening, and why. Thank God that Tony recovered!

We returned to Arizona, back to our lives. But again, my family suffered another loss – I had to fly back to Florida to bury my father. He could not live without my mom. He died only 63 days after her, at 93. How did I survive so many losses? How can one grieve so much? I had to choose courage.

Tony the Superstar

I was very close to Tony – he and I understood each other so well. He had many health issues due to his excess weight. In our family we all struggle with weight, and he had multiple complications due to his gastrointestinal surgeries. He was in emotional and physical pain.

In 2017, while we were living in Arizona, Tony told me that he was not feeling well. I wanted to take him to the doctor, but he did not want to go. He thought he was going to feel better the next day. We were alone in the house, and we went to sleep.

The plan was to take him to the hospital in the morning if he still did not feel well.

The plan failed.

I woke up in the morning, walked to the bathroom, and it was too late. I found him sitting on the floor, dead. He was silent and still. I sat with him and held him for hours. The two of us waited for the right moment to call my family. My family was celebrating Easter, which was a special day in our family.

The silence was all we had.

Tony was larger than life – a tall comedian, full of tattoos. He was a great uncle to Tyler's baby and they had a special bond. All the other children knew Tony growing up, and everyone wanted to meet me because of him. I was "Tony's mom." He and I were very connected, maybe because he was a giant "mini-me." We challenged each other and were each other's mirror. He did my grocery shopping and liked to go out to breakfast with me.

After his death, I felt like I had died too. My world lost its color and flavor. I miss him so much. He was such a good guy – a superman and my superstar! Tony's spirit has never left my side; I feel his presence with me all of the time. I really feel that he has found true peace; I want to believe that all my children are in heaven.

What my family went through is difficult to describe – painfully real, or surreal. No one in this world should go through as

The SHEro Mindset

much grief as we have, or continue to go through as much grief as I still face every day. To lose a child is the most painful of experiences. It rips your heart apart; it tears your mind and breaks your spirit.

The Ruins

During my travels, I saw many ancient buildings with amazing architecture: palaces, castles, temples. I was always intrigued by their history – especially the ruins in Turkey, Greece and Italy. Some were barely standing. The stories of what they endured to survive – war, natural disasters and time – had such an impact on me. These magnificent structures were built as places to live, worship and rule. The people in them must have experienced the spectrum of emotions – including anger, joy and fear – as they lived and loved. There were generations of humans celebrating, crying for their losses, and living in what time has turned to ruins.

The ruins remind us of the past – and like those ruins, I have been through disasters. At times, I was barely standing. But like the ancient Parthenon, I am more beautiful because of what I have endured. It makes me think... Does our past define us, or can we become beautiful – not despite, but because of, the challenges we have experienced?

After losing my children, I didn't care if the plane I was on went down, or if I jumped off a cliff and hit the bottom. I had no more fear, but I was exhausted and could not handle life anymore. I knew I needed to turn the situation around, so I went everywhere to find help. I read many self-help books; I learned about the afterlife; I went to Al-Anon and other support groups. I learned coping mechanisms and changed the way I thought, as well as how I felt.

My mindset is different now. My children and my parents are always with me. I feel them. Not like I did in life; it is a gentler sensation. Like the worn columns of the Parthenon in Athens that are not as complete as they once were, what is missing is filled with space, and the space frames the beauty of what is left. So it is with my loved ones who have passed. I found this truth over time, through psychics, by reading books, and from the wisdom of different religions and philosophies. I know that I'm going to be there one day with them, even if I don't know where "there" is. I hope it is nothing but heaven.

I have encountered many obstacles, and although they keep coming, it has helped me become stronger. I am sad for my living children, because they are still hurting. But I must let them work it out. As much as I want to change their thinking, I can't make them become the people that I think they should be.

I decided that I need to remain emotionally stable and say yes to happiness. I need to let the light shine on my wounds and heal. The hardest choice of my life has been the one to remain sane, despite the insanity that I have lived through. I did that by forgiving – forgiving myself, forgiving my children, forgiving Scott, and forgiving God. It doesn't have to be all black or white – in life, there are a lot of gray areas. I have decided to live my best life – to spend my time with happy thoughts. I know now that everything is in divine order. What if something wonderful happens out of all this loss?

Endless Love

Through these last 20 years, I have come to understand that first comes the lessons, then the knowledge, and third the discipline to practice the lessons. I am learning to love myself unconditionally. It sounds simple, but it is not; it is hard, and I remind myself often. If something challenges me, I know it is easy to go back into the dark, to the old patterns, and be depressed. It is easy to lose faith and hope when you are in the dark. Therefore, I keep choosing love. I must keep myself grounded, despite the insanity that goes on in my life. In all circumstances, I choose love.

Part of unconditional self-love is learning to feel safe with myself. Now I know that I can count on myself. I can be my own best friend. I can be my own mother and my own father. I can be my own sister and my own brother. I must love myself unconditionally – it is the only way to make it through this journey. We come alone and we die alone, but while we are here, we can enjoy each other and the miracle of the present moment. It is the only thing we have.

Tragedy taught me to know the depths of my own heart. No matter how much my heart hurts, I know now that I can find joy and bring peace back into my life. I am the one who chooses how I respond to life and what kind of person I'm going to be. I can't have anyone else do that for me. In a way, it's like going back to parenting a little girl. I must love that little girl, because if I don't take care of her, she'll be all alone. She doesn't know how to take care of herself yet.

I have learned that people come and go in our lives. They can walk the same path we do for a time, but one day they will not be there anymore. I am a people person, and I must be with people to be happy. I have learned how to make new friends. It took me some time, but that is what I want as this new woman that I am becoming.

If I had to relive everything I went through again to be the mother of my six children, I would do it in a heartbeat. I remember the good times that we had with Nick, Tyler, Madison and Tony. They were my children – they **are** my children, and they always will be.

Heaven or earth, my Stars will always be with me. I have loved ones in heaven, and I am grateful to go on living my life here on earth.

One day, my spirit will be free to soar and reunite with my Stars in heaven. Until then, I have a life to live and a purpose to fulfill. My wish is to inspire someone who is struggling to survive to have courage, and to comfort someone who is suffering loss.

A New Beginning

I know I have a purpose in life. Now I also know that there is always a new beginning, and room to repair old connections if love remains in your heart. Scott and I decided to give each other a second chance. We married again in 2018 on the anniversary of our first marriage. It was a beautiful ceremony – just the two of us on the island of St. Lucia. The foliage was so green and lush; we could hear the waves of the Caribbean Sea in the background. It was such a gentle and kind day. Our longing to be together was, and is, forever in our hearts and souls. When we arrived back home, we had an amazing reception with our friends and family. Everyone was so happy, including the bride and groom!

We are like the cowardly lion and the heartless tin man in the Wizard of Oz. The courage has always been there, and the heart has been too. I made the decision to be happy, despite everything. It takes courage to dream again. This is my SHEro mindset.

I am thankful to my family and friends, from kindergarten through the present day, who have lightened my burdens by being there for me and by acknowledging my children's existence. I'd also like to acknowledge my group of Compassionate Friends (parents of children that have passed). They have taught me that true happiness can be found through the eyes of others who have traveled this journey alongside me.

Bon Voyage

If I had to choose a future vision of my life, I would spend time with my family in France during the springtime. Paris and Chamonix are my favorite places to be – not too cold, not too hot, just perfect. I see it so clearly:

The trees and plants are blooming and showing off their beauty in every corner of my favorite place. We are in Les Jardins de Talèfre in Chamonix. My grandchildren are running on the grass, and the rest of us are sitting and enjoying each other's company.

We are having a small picnic of French cheese on baguettes with dried fruit. Scott and I are sitting together – we are old and in love. My family is smiling and savoring our time together. The grandchildren are playing. Classical music is playing in the background and the garden is full of flowers.

People are walking by, both tourists and locals. Some are lying down, enjoying the sun and eating delicious food. It is a calm place to enjoy family, surrounded by beautiful architecture.

I am peaceful, content, and I feel complete in my future vision. I have my dreams back, and life can still be extraordinary. I have hope. I can be happy again… because I understand that there is no separation.

As it says in *The Little Prince*, "And now here is my secret… it is only with the heart that one can see rightly; what is essential is invisible to the eye."

— SUZY NANIA

Inspiration to Live Courageously

In life, we often focus on the verbs to do and to have, but *The SHEro Mindset* is about practicing the verb to BE. Use these suggestions to live courageously.

Be Brave
Courage is an energy that comes from your heart. Stand up for yourself; stand up for others. Bravery allows you to navigate life with peace in your heart. Connect to your power, so that you can use the energy of courage to make changes.

Be Wise
Courage requires wisdom in your choices. When you apply your intention and act to make a difference, you can create change. This is what wisdom looks like.

Find Motivation
What motivates you to have courage? Fear may still be present in your life, and you will need to conquer that fear to act. Many times, a loved one will need us to have courage. Staying motivated is the best way to achieve your goals.

Be Inspired
What inspires you? When you find that person, story or thing that inspires you, courage comes naturally. Saying yes to life, to opportunities, is fundamental. Not everything will come easily in our lives, but we can be inspired, especially by our heroes. Inspiration leads to courage.

Courage Meditation

Choose courage over fear,
Find courage in your heart and soul
Find acceptance in the middle of chaos,
and the energy to seek the light...
Be grateful for life; and honor who you are,
even if you don't fit into the normal box.
Remain sane when the world is crumbling...
And learn how to love yourself unconditionally.
Make new friends who accept you just the way you are.
Have the courage to carry on old traditions
and rituals that otherwise might be forgotten.
Face the night terrors that haunt us all.
Stay calm and safe in your heart.
Understand your value, your purpose.
Chose to live in a constant state of love.
Because where there is love... there is no fear.
May your life be peaceful, and your days be joyful.
May our stories not define us, and may our spirits soar freely.
May God protect us as the angels remind us to breathe.

SUZY NANIA

The Power of
CREATIVITY

Our positive creations connect us to our source, to our creator. Creativity can bring us solutions, enlightenment, innovation and development. When we are flowing creativity, our brain is pure light vibrating with the cosmos. We can experience the flow of life. We become one with nature, as nature is constantly creating… it gives us the freedom to express ourselves and at the same time be in the present moment. It gives us the tools to heal from the deepest places of our soul.

*Creativity is a unique way of seeing,
being, and acting that is distinctively ours.
It involves producing ideas or behaviors that are
original, useful, and powerful resources.
Always present, it is a character strength
that can help us solve problems,
experience life with joy,
and make a positive contribution
to our life and the lives of others.*

NANCY KIRSNER

CHAPTER 6

Creativity

The virtue of creativity can be a powerful tool to help one thrive. Alexia (nicknamed Biro) is a talented artist with a wonderful story. Some people may call it serendipity, but I know that Alexia and I were destined to meet and become best friends. I also know it is not a coincidence that I am writing the introduction to her chapter in Paris – the City of Lights and a city of the arts – and the place Alexia was born.

How did I meet Alexia? Let me tell you... I remember it as if it were yesterday. It was a normal day at the House of Gaia. Alexia and her companion were both curious about our programs. They were trying to find some art activities and a place where Alexia could flourish, so they came for a visit.

When they asked about our mission, I told them about our art curriculum and our social inclusion program. I described the many opportunities Alexia would have to shine her light and experience life in our community. I could see that Alexia was excited to have found us. Her eyes were bright, and she was smiling! I was happy she had found us too.

I instantly knew that our individual purposes were aligned, and that together, we could build bridges and close the gap

The SHEro Mindset

between people with different abilities. Alexia's visit that afternoon confirmed to me that I was in the right space at the right time, doing the right thing. I was creating a space where every human could be accepted and respected as equal, while experiencing endless possibilities for meaningful connection. Our center was exactly what Alexia was looking for in Naples: a safe, welcoming and creative space. A happy place!

Alexia inspires me every day to be a better person, and to be as grateful for my life as she is for hers. During the past 10 years, I have seen her: thrive through her art; publish a book; become a speaker; and travel the world. Alexia is a valued member of our community who is courageous, generous, and kind. I am so incredibly proud of her achievements.

In the following pages, Alexia will share how she has transformed every single struggle into a positive life lesson. She will tell you about the importance of a positive mindset and how she developed the tools to cope with her physical challenges and limitations. I invite you to read this SHEro's journey of Creativity and I welcome you to Biro's world!

— LULU

Alexia's Story
The Can-Do Attitude

In 1981, in the early morning hours of a spring day, a beautiful baby was born at the American Hospital of Paris. That baby, named Alexia, was me – the first child born into my family. My mother's pregnancy was happy and healthy, and the birth was smooth and normal. I was such a cute baby.

A Child with No Tears

But despite all of this, something was very wrong with me.

The doctors were concerned about my health, and decided to keep me at the hospital for a month to run more tests. As time went by, they saw things that concerned them: when I bit through my tongue, I felt no pain; when I swallowed, I spit up; and when I cried, there were no tears.

A child with no tears? How was it possible?

My parents' lives were changed forever because they were determined to find the reason why I was not like other babies. They had so many questions: How long would I live? Would I choke the next time I tried to swallow milk? What would my life be like? What kind of parents would they have to be for me? How could they address my needs?

They just wanted to raise me with love, health and happiness. But at that time there were so many unknowns and there was so much fear. It took two years for the doctors to finally figure out what I had – a very rare hereditary condition, called familial dysautonomia (FD).

Pause...

My parents had never heard of familial dysautonomia. They went above and beyond to understand FD. I was the only case in France, and no one really knew what to do. You have probably never met a person with my disability. There are very few of us.

FD is where the nerve endings in the body are not fully developed. FD is progressive and affects the optic nerve and balance. Over time, swallowing became an issue, causing some food and liquids to go into my lungs. That created aspiration pneumonia. Aspiration pneumonia is the main reason that those with FD pass away at an early age.

My parents were vigilant, and so careful about my well-being. I became my parents' porcelain doll – I was fragile, yet curious and energetic. In my parents' eyes, I was the perfect daughter. In fact, people would stop my parents to comment about how cute I was, with big blue eyes and thick, wavy, brown hair. No one knew much about my condition or what kind of life I was going to live.

To Feel or Not to Feel

When I turned two, my parents decided to have another baby – it was a boy. I was so little, but I still remember being excited by the birth of my brother, Greg. After he was born, my life would never be the same. I knew he would always be there for me, no matter what.

We were inseparable! Greg was always wonderful with me, cuddling me, teasing me, playing tricks on me. In his presence, I was happy and acted playful, like any other child. One time, when we were young, we were playing around on my parents' bed, and Greg accidentally pulled out my feeding tube. We were two children just enjoying time together... I still tease him about it!

There are so many stories about growing up together that I could write a whole book. One time I lost my retainer, and even though we searched everywhere in the apartment, we could not find it. Finally, Greg figured out that I had accidentally swallowed it but couldn't feel it! He saved me by letting my parents know and so they could rush me to the hospital. My life was a series of challenges – and still is.

Sometimes FD causes learning disabilities, but those with FD often have above average memory and aptitude, especially for visual games and puzzles. Growing up, I was great at video games, especially Super Mario and other Nintendo games. And I could put together a puzzle more quickly than anyone! Unfortunately, people still underestimate our intelligence and abilities, and some don't even know how to engage with us.

Even though I may have looked normal on the outside, I did not quite fit in with other children in my school. During my time in elementary school in Paris, other students bullied me because I acted differently. I made coughing noises and I moved more slowly than the other children. So, every day, after an hour of school, I would pretend to be sick, by coughing and gagging. Then my great-grandmother would come pick me up. I did not want to be in school, having to endure the mean children. I just wanted to be home, where I felt normal and loved by my family; I wanted to be in a place that felt safe.

While I could not feel my body, I could feel emotions, and I had to learn how to cope with them. My emotions were deep. I was a good child, sensitive and creative, and I did not want to be seen as the sick child at school. Rather, I wanted to be loved by friends and be accepted for who I was, like I was at home. My family supported me and helped me so much growing up.

I have many great memories of my childhood in Europe. My father, Gerard, and I have a special bond. Dad was fun and creative, and he always encouraged my brother and me to be our own selves. He was more than a father; he was my coach and teacher. He taught me the most meaningful lessons about self-esteem and to love myself unconditionally.

One of my favorite times was when my dad drove my brother and me to school. He wanted us to have a love for learning, so he would create a theme for our ride to school. Dad called it the "rolling school," and every morning, there was a new lesson. Dad would ask us questions, like: "What is the significance of a certain river running through Paris? What is the world's largest museum, and why is it in this city?"

That car ride was the highlight of the day, and I learned more there than I ever did in school. I especially absorbed what my dad always told me, "There's nothing you can't do." It sunk in and I believed it.

Seeking a Healthier Life

Our journey to find answers for my treatment led us to New York City, where there was a center specializing in FD. In 1990, we moved to New York City from Paris. I was nearly 10 years old, and I needed the best medical care for my condition. Around this time, something else also changed in my life – my parents separated from each other. Our move marked new beginnings for all of us. So even though my parents were not together anymore, I was excited about what life could bring.

My mother, Carol, was very focused on my medical needs and education, and one day she met a lady who changed my life. The lady told us about a fantastic public school called P.S. 234 for people with disabilities. I met my best friend Xian there. She also had a great attitude, despite having had cerebral palsy as a child, which required her to walk with poles. I really admired Xian for being positive, bright and fun. I remember meeting her in the lunchroom when I was in fourth grade. She lived nearby, so we would have sleepovers and movie nights all the time! Sadly, after junior high we lost touch for a long time.

Another thing I loved about my years in New York was going to museums one-on-one with my stepfather, Fred. Both he and my mom are passionate about art, and it rubbed off on me.

Overcoming My Fears

When I was 17 years old, I moved to London with my father and stepmother, Brooke. Yes, both of my parents had remarried, and I was happy for them. I was blessed with two parents and two wonderful stepparents. Brooke and Fred really support my creativity, and they constantly give me praise for my achievements!

Even though I was looking forward to moving back to Europe, I still had to face many challenges as I tried to be more independent. When we first arrived, it was always drizzling, and my greatest fear was wet leaves – I didn't want to slip and fall. I was so afraid of hurting myself. As I got older, my balance became progressively worse, and eventually I ended up needing a walker.

For a few years, I had to have someone with me when I left the house. I became tired and frustrated with that situation. I was young and full of energy, and I wanted to be free to go out alone. I was determined to change my life. I asked my parents to give me a chance to prove I could be more independent. They were nervous about my decision, but they were also supportive and allowed me to be trained by my occupational therapist.

I confronted my fear, and every day I learned a little bit more about myself. It took me a year to learn how to cross the street by myself. Finally, I was free! I was so empowered by knowing

Creativity

how to go out alone that I really felt I could do anything. I was proud of myself and shared my experience with everyone.

Life became manageable. I was ready to learn about everything. I learned to take the bus everywhere because it was accessible for people with walkers, wheelchairs, and different physical abilities. I used to take the bus nearly every day. I was experiencing freedom; I could go anywhere I wanted to go. I was young and alive!

These victories were big morale boosters! Bit by bit, my self-esteem grew. The more I did on my own, the less scary it became. If I failed or became afraid, the next day I tried again. I taught myself to "Just Do It!" – whatever the challenge.

I had always loved horses, and after some time in London, I decided that I wanted to ride (even though this sounded almost impossible with my poor balance). We found a program in the Royal Mews, attached to Buckingham Palace, which was free for anyone with a disability. It was led by the captain of the Guard. The very first time I rode, I did figure-eights! I felt so powerful as the horse's legs became mine; suddenly, I was better than normal. I felt like a super woman.

All these experiences gave me more self-esteem and made me feel proud of myself.

The Whispers of My Soul

The encouragement I received from my parents gave me the attitude I have today. My mother says, "You are a warrior, not a worrier." But I often think, *What would happen to me if I didn't have their support? How would I be?*

Yes, my parents encouraged me, but what gave me my mindset was something unique and special that came from deep inside. It came from my heart, from my soul, from my faith, from keeping a perspective about life, and from not spending time with negative thoughts. I created my own mindset. For me, the sky had no limits.

The Love of Learning

I wanted to evolve my life even more by going to university. I was not so sure if I could, but I did anyway. In London, I attended the American Intercontinental University (AIU) and studied visual communication and graphic design. I had a note-taker in class and was given extra time on exams, but I took all the same tests as the other students.

After living at home with my dad and stepmother for the first couple of years of university, I felt that I wanted to live on my own in a student housing facility. That really panicked my parents; but as they normally do, they supported me. I was ready to expand my horizons even further!

To everyone's amazement (including my own), after six years, I graduated! It took me a little longer, but I didn't mind going at my own pace. During my graduation, when the diploma was presented to me as I stood with my walker, the whole audience stood and applauded! I felt so surprised, and overwhelmed with joy.

It was one of the best moments of my life. I had worked so hard, overcome so many challenges, and finally I could celebrate! The night of my graduation, I organized a party with twinkling lights under the stars on the roof of a restaurant. I invited every person who had ever helped me in any way, even with just a kind word – from the lady at the coffee shop to the flower man on our street. The place was packed!

The time on my own at university was important. It was a transformative experience; it enabled me to really cope with my limitations but also to recognize my abilities. I developed great friendships with students my own age from all different countries. I was able to go out and come home as I wished, on foot with my walker or with public transportation. It was very cool for me to do things that most people take for granted. I didn't feel disabled, because I could do what I wanted, when I wanted. Living on my own was a huge victory, and finally I felt totally independent!

Not only did I learn how to do these things, but I participated in a 5K run in Regent's Park in London. Can you imagine? I had to commit myself to train for that for hours – confronting my fears, and enduring the danger of the rain and snow. But I did it!

The Art of Happiness

Motivated by becoming a graphic designer and by participating in the marathon, I was ready to share my story. So, I decided to write and illustrate a book. My book was meant to empower everyone with my can-do attitude. I described a lot of my challenges in the book, which I titled *Steps of Life: Exceeding Boundaries*. The book project was a collaboration with my tutor and my family. In fact, my life was very much influenced by all of the people who helped me to achieve my dreams.

Let me share an excerpt from my book, which explains how I felt when I simply learned to cross the street:

I am at the crosswalk.

There are big yellow lights flashing on and off over my head warning of traffic.

I am sweating.

I imagine the cars are racing.

The distance from here to the other side seems huge.

I turn my head from side to side, then wait until the cars stop before I cross.

This is the very first time I have to do this alone and I am panicked.

My body is shaking, and I feel stiff and hot.

My hands are tight on the handle grips of the walker.

Despite the fear, I was not inhibited from pursuing my purpose. I was overjoyed when the book was published. So many people told me that they were inspired by my story and realized that they, too, could overcome their fears and challenges. We all can. We are made to be overcomers.

Creativity

Finding a Place of Inclusion

In 2011, my dad and stepmom moved to Naples, Florida. I wasn't ready to leave London yet, because I wanted more time in the world that I had created with my friends. I also wanted to finish my book. A built-in support network was already in place in London, so it all worked for me to stay there. But after a year, I decided to move to Florida to be close to my family and enjoy the warm weather.

When I first arrived in Florida, I stayed in an independent living facility called the Carlisle, with mostly older people. I was the youngest person there. At first, I enjoyed all the nice activities, but over time I became upset, because the friends I made were much older than I was – and they kept passing away. The place was nice, but I could not quite call it home.

The best thing about living at the Carlisle was meeting my dance teacher, Corey. He believed in me and encouraged me to participate in ballroom dance lessons. I haven't forgotten how great it made me feel! Somehow, he was not afraid of me falling. He took risks with his movements and held my body so carefully. I felt alive – as if I was flying.

I was still so young. I needed another life, especially after Corey left. One of my assistants did some research, and found a unique and creative place called House of Gaia. It was a local nonprofit community center. I did not know what to expect, other than knowing that I could take some art classes there.

When I arrived there, I liked the space. It was very colorful and cheerful. I met Lulu, the founder and president of the nonprofit. She had a vision of social inclusion, and I loved her because of that. She could see me – beyond my disabilities. She understood me 100 percent and I did not have to explain to her why I was there.

She had big plans for me. But wisely, she gently eased me into their activities.

Lulu and I had so many things in common. We both studied the same subject at university; we shared a love of art. She had traveled to Europe many times, and we could talk about that. I met her mother Lis and her stepfather Roberto; they were always so happy to see me, and they welcomed me with big smiles on their faces.

At House of Gaia, I was blossoming again. I was invited by many members to go out. I had a special fairytale birthday party. House of Gaia became my place to go in our community. I became Lulu's SHEro, as she became mine. We mentor and inspire each other.

My Expression

Sometimes it's hard for me to find the right words to express myself. I feel so much and so deeply that words are not adequate. I find that I can express myself so much better through art and other creative activities than through words. Painting, dancing, swimming, prayer, and laughter all allow me to express myself and to uplift people around me.

Just because I don't have tears, it doesn't mean I don't have intense emotions. I can pour all my feelings into my art, together with prayers for health, joy, love and fulfillment – which people say they can feel.

My art is my identity. I am an artist. I love to express my feelings on the canvas, and I want to share my joy with everyone through my paintings.

Dealing With Being Alone

Before the pandemic, I was enjoying my life. I was starting to socialize, make friends, and live my dreams when everything shut down. The fear of having COVID-19 or losing my friends or loved ones became a big concern for me. I could not take any chances with FD. To protect myself from the virus, I isolated myself and had to learn how to live inside an apartment again. I had to learn how to adapt to the new reality, like most people did.

Being isolated during this time has been tough for me, because I am a very social person. But thank God, I made it to this point by being surrounded by my parents, my brother, his super wife Stephanie, and my baby niece and godchild Lea. And I was so thankful for my friends – who met with me using the Zoom app, called me on the phone, and sent texts. I also love practicing yoga over Zoom with Mrs. Salima, a teacher I met through House of Gaia.

I may be alone, but I am not a loner. I have my art. I know I am loved, and I know I have people who care for me. I have to believe that this moment, too, shall pass. I have hope that soon I will be reunited in person with the ones who make me happy, and that I'll be able to resume achieving my dreams and serving my purpose.

The SHEro's Gratitude

On March 7, 2021, I had my 40th birthday. It was a major celebration of gratitude, especially because I have FD. When I was born, those with FD weren't expected to live to my age; they passed away from pneumonia or other problems before becoming teenagers. I am one of only 350 people in the entire world with FD.

So, my 40th birthday was a real milestone.

I understand that my condition is part of who I am as a person. I am enriched by lessons I have learned through my limitations. All the challenges helped me to become my best self. I am no victim; I don't act like one. Instead, I realize how fortunate and blessed I am to be alive, and to be able to participate in this life and serve my purpose.

I understand the importance of acceptance. When someone is faced with a physical or mental challenge that affects functions, like talking, swallowing, walking or seeing, they need to go deeper into themselves and find self-compassion.

I think complaining about life is such a waste of time and energy. Instead, I am focused on gratitude, for the wonderful opportunities I have. I am so thankful for all the people that

Creativity

I have met who I learned from, and also for those I taught about being positive in life.

I have to share that God also reunited me with one of my best friends, Xian, from my elementary school in New York. Through social media and the efforts of my beloved pastor, I found her again. She is an amazing person who spreads so much joy. We are now inseparable!

Xian says, "It's a blessing to be in Alexia's life because she loves the way a waterfall flows; both calming and relentlessly powerful, beautiful to behold. She happily pours out all she has to give the world unwavering positive energy. She's such a role model to those around her, because her love is unapologetic and overflowing. She can move mountains with ease and joy, and does so daily."

My Superpowers

My attitude, my willpower, my ability to listen and to cheer people up, my joy, my peacefulness and my love are my superpowers. We are all born with qualities like these, and we can all enjoy them if we choose. I simply made the choice. My creativity is also a great superpower that has allowed me to live an amazing life.

My greatest superpower is that I know God is in me and with me. I can pray, I can love, and I can praise and thank Him for all my blessings. We all have that same superpower. God is in every person, and we can all do these things. We are all His children.

We are all born with gifts, and we all have to unleash our gifts upon the world.

I used to be incredibly shy and had difficulty speaking to people, but when I began to deepen my faith, I felt comfortable talking more and more. I speak and pray to God. I ask Him to help people to feel better, to improve their lives in all different ways, and to increase my strength and my peace.

My faith helps to lift me up when I need help, so I can lift up others. Communicating with God is so special and wonderful. I'm never alone anymore. I am constantly surrounded by Him.

I Live to Inspire

I am proud to share with you my SHEro story. My journey is not over, even though every day I still have many challenges. I am now legally blind, but I am still pursuing everything I love. And creativity powers so much of my life.

I am grateful that I have had the opportunity to see so many beautiful things in the world! I still hold the memories of all that beauty in my heart and mind. I appreciate my life lessons; every single struggle has pushed me to the next level. I am stronger today, and I am in love with life. I still paint and produce art. I still have dreams and hope for my future.

My disability helps people to feel comfortable with me, and to open up and share about their situations. So, I see my condition as a good thing. I love people and connect with them on a deep level. I want to be a blessing for each person

I'm with, friend or stranger. I encourage people to go on in life, finding their joy and being grateful for who they are.

My purpose in life is to inspire others to just keep going! My stepmother says, "Alexia is an amazing inspiration and has enriched my life! On the one hand, she is like an angel – incredibly kind, always happy, and life-affirming. She is also exceptionally strong, courageous, and perseverant. When she sets her mind on something, just get out of the way! Even if it doesn't seem possible, she's going to try to do it!"

I walk the talk about what I preach. My message is that you need to love yourself – by accepting yourself, believing in yourself, staying positive, being the best that you can be, and having a lot of compassion for yourself. Remember that there is only one of you who will ever exist, and God has made you just the way He wants you to be for His plan.

You have to confront your fears; you have to be brave and seek freedom of expression. By simply understanding that nothing can prevent you from having a good life, you can truly be happier.

I hope my story gives you the boost you need to realize your dreams. You can create your life like I created mine – by using creativity! So, go on – what are you waiting for?

— ALEXIA DE GUNZBURG

Inspiration to Be Creative

In life, we often focus on the verbs to do and to have, but *The SHEro Mindset* is about practicing the verb to BE. Use these affirmations to express the creativity of a SHEro.

Be Bold

We are here to live, and hopefully to leave our mark. Dimming your light won't help anyone. When you shine, you show others that they can too. Sometimes we need to take risks to create. Our boldness empowers others to do the same.

Be Curious

Your curiosity can lead you to learn new things, find answers, and create something that did not exist before. A curious person can be creative and find new ways to express themselves. Play with your creativity through your curiosity.

Be Imaginative

Your mind is powerful, and imagination has the power to create a world full of possibilities.

You were born to create! As a baby, you developed your brain by role-playing and by being imaginative. Recapture the imagination that you had as a child, so that you can create as an adult.

Be Inclusive

The universe is always creating something new and letting go of other things. When we include others, we come into sync with the universe. The planets are not alone; they have each other. Even as far away as the sun and the moon are from us, they play a role in our lives. You can create your own universe when you are inclusive.

Creativity Meditation

I am a creator
I have used my imagination.
By changing my perspective of things,
Things can adjust to new reality
And unfold into something new.
Life is transformative
Things are never the same.
By being creative
I can be inventive, wiser, and more…
Spontaneous
Art brings me to the moment
I can use art in everything I do and touch.
I can close my eyes
And I can imagine positive things
Happening to me and others.
I can connect to my higher power
With more fluidity by being creative.
The creative path allows more freedom
In my life, I can experience the flow
Creativity
Gives me more opportunities to find more
Solutions to my problems.
It helps me to transcend
And to escape the darkness.
We are all born artists,
All born creators.
So express yourself with love,
With compassion and kindness.
Create the world you want to live in.

The Power of
FAITH

Who am I, if I am not my Faith? Who am I, if I don't have anything to believe in, something to pursue, or someone to follow or lead? We are all connected to this earth by breathing the same air, by feeling the warmth of the sun, by sharing the same heartbeat. Faith and hope merge, giving us the courage to: go on in life, overcome our troubles, learn from the lessons, and befriend our fears. For some, faith comes from God, Buddha, Shiva or another deity or life source. Faith can be found in our higher self or from trusting something larger than ourselves, something that makes us transcend. Faith is a virtue that has an incredible power to keep us alive.

*Faith is the foundation of our life.
Not faith in our world, not in government,
not in circumstances, not in others.
Faith outside of us is changeable and uncontrollable,
where life can change in a moment.
The faith is in God, in our strength,
 hope, passion, and in our destiny.
With God, all things are possible.*

MARY BELLOFATTO

CHAPTER 7
Faith

Didi came to my life through our nonprofit outreach program and was introduced to me by a mutual colleague, Kristin. At the time, Didi was working for a Title I school. Together with Kristin, we wanted to create community art to help tell the story of immigrant parents at a Title I school in a very underprivileged area of our county.

My connection with Didi was instant. We share the same love of education and travel, and we both admire other cultures. Didi immediately understood our nonprofit mission focused on inclusion, social justice, and the celebration of diversity. Our nonprofit began to collect donations to help support the families of Didi's school. My mother was involved in the project as well, and the four of us delivered the most amazing quilt to the school as part of the project.

Kristin invited Didi and her husband Alberto, along with Adam and me, to her house to share in a special moment with her family and have a delicious lunch. Kristin's husband Alex is a chef from Barcelona and a specialist in paella – a rich dish with lots of seafood on a bed of yellow rice. We had a very relaxing time, and shared a lot of joy together.

The SHEro Mindset

We started to follow each other on Facebook and stayed connected through social media. Didi liked my posts and I liked hers. I could see her love for her family and her appreciation of beauty in her posts. I enjoyed seeing pictures of her road trips with her boys and husband. They are a very close family, and the images of her experiences always brought joy to my heart.

In 2019, Didi started to share something very profound that happened to her (which she also shares in depth in this book). By observing how her story developed on social media, I started to feel closer to her. I developed tremendous admiration for her; she became a role model for so many, as well as my SHEro.

What Didi calls energy and love, I call Faith. And it is above and beyond what I have seen before – she inspires me and others so much. Her strength, tenacity and endurance push the limits of life. Didi determines her destiny as she writes her stories.

Didi represents Faith not in the religious sense, but in her confidence, trust and hope. It is beautiful to hear her words of optimism and how she chose to go through her challenges and hard shifts. Her chapter reveals a very realistic woman who surrenders to her visual meditation and chooses her voice over science.

— LULU

Didi's Story
Life Is What You Make It

I was born on Long Island and grew up in Rochester, New York. I come from a very dysfunctional family, and so from the age of 7, music helped me escape from a violent, caustic environment at home. Music for me was my saving grace. By the time I was in middle school, I was traveling with the Rochester Philharmonic Youth Orchestra. I learned that through hard work and dedication, one could decide their own destiny instead of accepting what others dished out. In music, I found a source of joy.

I spent countless hours practicing to earn the honor of being in groups that took me away from the terrible dysfunction that was killing my spirit. Learning and practicing refueled me, and empowered me to share music with others. If you have ever played an instrument, you know that music is an extension of your soul. Playing an instrument is a chance to express the elation, as well as the pain, of who you are, and to share your triumph over pain through your instrument.

When I was 17, I went to Boston University and then I transferred to the New England Conservatory, where I played the oboe. Music became my refuge and created a wellspring of determination in me, and a resilience that would be essential for my survival.

My Rock

In 1990, when I was 19 years old, I went to Spain to visit my sister Mary at Christmas time. She was studying in Madrid, and since we have always been close, I decided I would surprise her with a visit. It was during that visit that I met Alberto, the man who would become an integral part of my life's journey.

My sister and her boyfriend introduced me to nearly all of their friends, but were not going to introduce me to Alberto, because he was so quiet and I was always so extroverted. Alberto and I finally met on New Year's Eve, because my sister's boyfriend (now my brother-in-law) was very good friends with Alberto and his family, and always spent New Year's Eve with them at their house. I was invited along since I was visiting. I saw Alberto across the room, he smiled at me, and I felt like I had met my twin soul.

In his smile, there was a warmth that was palpable. His eyes reflected an incredible strength and understanding. During the two weeks I was there, he was the only one who really tried to communicate with me – which was difficult, since he didn't speak English and I didn't speak Spanish. We managed to understand each other with the help of a pocket-sized Spanish-English dictionary, and I knew that someday I would marry him.

In 1992, I returned to Spain for my sister's wedding. And just like that, I met Alberto again at my sister's party. The connection continued to grow, even though we were still not fluent in each other's language.

At this time, I was studying at the New England Conservatory, working three jobs to pay for my schooling. I needed a break. My sister suggested that I stay in Spain for a while to allow myself some time to decide where my future was headed. I decided to stay if I could find a job; and with my sister's help, I found two jobs: one teaching English and the other being the nanny for Alberto's nephews. This was the perfect opportunity for me to learn Spanish so that I could finally speak to Alberto and discover if our relationship was possible.

The Sound of Happiness

I left a solid job as a music teacher to move to Spain to work as an English teacher at a small academy.

In March 2001, Alberto and I finally got married, and that changed everything. I was able to find a job as an English teacher with the Comunidad de Madrid and we were finally settled enough to start a family.

I was so excited to be pregnant, but because I was high-risk, I had to stay in bed and take a break from playing. I was five months pregnant with my first son when I was finally allowed to play music again.

I was so nervous because the baby had not moved. I went to the doctor and explained my concerns, and he assured me that he could hear the baby's heartbeat. He asked me about my vocation, and I explained that I was playing in a Baroque chamber orchestra.

He laughed and told me that the baby probably hadn't moved yet because he was bored! That dispelled my fears, and I continued playing. I was so happy to share my love of music with my unborn child. Now I had the best of both worlds – my intense love of music and my undying love for my child.

Music was such a part of our lives. The baby started moving when I was playing a concert which featured Beethoven's Ninth Symphony. The chorus came in and he started kicking vigorously, so much so that my oboe was moving off my belly. I am convinced that the energy generated by that beautiful music, shared by so many musicians with the audience, inspired my baby.

Two months later, Ander was born, and he became our orchestra mascot. Alberto brought him to all of my concerts, and he quietly absorbed the music, never crying.

Our other son, Nicolas, came 16 months later. It was the same story; both of my pregnancies were high-risk. So I faced more bed rest, and another sabbatical from playing the oboe. Nicolas was born a month early, just like Ander, and I had a team of neonatal specialists on hand. He was not absorbing oxygen, and was taken away from me right away.

The doctors put him under special lights for a half hour, and he still was not absorbing enough oxygen. A midwife, who was also involved in the birth, took Nicolas from under the lights and said, "What this baby needs is the warmth of his mother."

The Heroes Before the SHEro

Life has not been easy for my family at times. We have faced many challenges, but nothing was as terrifying as the day Ander was diagnosed with cancer. He was only 7 years old, but he was so mature for his age.

We were still living in Spain, and my husband had just lost his business. We were lost... I felt trapped... I had never ever experienced anything like that before. Ander was only 7 and his cancer was very aggressive. His fever would go up and down. I remember stroking his hair and meditating with him.

He said, "I wish it worked, Mom, but it is not working; meditation is not helping. I am in pain. Everything hurts..."

I took him right back to the hospital and they gave him morphine, which at times was the only thing that worked.

Ander was brave, and never complained. He always made sure I was fine; he did not want me to be sad. I saw my boy becoming his own hero... even with open lesions from his mouth to his bottom.

Nicolas was only 5 years old at the time. He was my hero too. But he almost lost his brother and he lost my presence in the house. He didn't understand when I returned home from the hospital without his brother. He would get very angry at me for leaving Ander in the hospital. It was so hard for me to explain to him everything that was going on with his best friend. At that point, I knew deep in my heart I had to change the dynamic and become their SHEro.

My SHEro Way

I had to change my mindset. Fear would destroy us. I was determined to help my boys, to save my marriage, and to lift my family out of all that pain and the hopeless feeling.

I did not make a big deal out of it. This was simply another part of our life. Being creative, I invented a game. It became our game.

We let our imagination take over our fears. We loved the Age of Empires game on the computer. So, we applied the rules of the game to Ander's treatment. Each chemo session had a color. The doctors were the ones fighting for him, just like in the Age of Empires. Anders was distracted with the game… but the pain never left. It was always there.

Nicolas gave me strength. Alberto gave me strength. Now I needed to give them mine and show my love. I needed to be strong for my boys.

Starting All Over Again

I had never planned on coming back to the United States. Madrid was my home and so I had let everything related to the States expire, including my teaching certificate. The situation in Spain in 2011 was bad. The recession had hit hard; that is why Alberto's company went under. We tried to hang on for a year, but it was just too much. I made the decision to come back to the US when we went grocery shopping and I couldn't afford to pay for the $40 worth of groceries.

That is how I grew up – leaving groceries on the conveyor belt and walking out of the store with my mom in shame, because we couldn't pay for them. I always swore that my children were not going to grow up like that, and so I made the decision to leave Spain.

It was not easy for Alberto to agree to that decision. He is very close with his family, and he had never thought about leaving Madrid. In fact, up until a week before we left, he was not sure that he was coming with us. I think he saw my determination and realized that the move was what our family needed in order to survive. I think he also saw that the move would provide opportunities for our children. In the end, he did come with us, and our family unit remained strong.

Leaving one's country because you must is not easy. You leave your language, culture, friends and family behind, and you venture into the unknown. Doing it with children is even more difficult. We had no money for extras, so we only brought what we could fit in our suitcases and two bike boxes. We left the rest of our life in storage or sold it to have money for the trip. The boys were able to choose a few favorite toys to bring with them. The majority of our items were left behind – Legos, books, stuffed animals, treasured collections, Christmas ornaments, and photo albums. It was a lifetime for them and 12 years for us.

Finding Closure

We said goodbye to our life in Spain and started on our new adventure in Florida. I am always amazed when I think about my children. They had to move at the ages of 8 and 6½, leaving everything they knew behind – and they did so without a single complaint.

I had to work two jobs to support us until Alberto could get residency and look for work. I used that situation as a teaching opportunity for our children. It was important to me that they understood that life's circumstances could change in an instant, but that with faith, we could make the best of it.

It is a waste of energy to complain or feel sorry for yourself. Rather, we need to find happy moments to hold onto when difficult times come. We found our solace in nature walks, in family game nights, and by practicing gratitude for what we were achieving as a family.

What Is Truly Important?

It was a difficult first year. Ander was still recovering from his bout with cancer, and we still had to take him to monthly medical visits. He also had to have his port removed. I was horrified when the hospital staff brought me to the business office to pay the bill before they would take care of my son. I couldn't believe the callousness. There was no understanding that my heart was with my son, who was supposed to be undergoing surgery.

There was only, "I'm sorry ma'am, but you can pay with a credit card if you don't have cash. We cannot begin the operation until the bill is settled." I remember looking at the woman, perplexed, thinking how unfortunate it was that she worked in a place that had stripped her humanity away.

I paid the bill, and was brought back to the OR to kiss my son before they put him under. He knew he was getting his port out, which meant no more chemo treatments. He was so relieved and happy.

His smile as I held his hand washed away the angst I had been feeling. I was once again reminded of what is truly important. My little hero was about to undergo his last surgery, which marked the end of his fight with cancer – a fight he had won; a fight we all had won. There was no greater joy than that. It had been a difficult year, but we made it together as a family, and we were so much stronger for it.

Once we were settled, things became easier. We wanted the boys to integrate into social settings as soon as possible, so we found various activities for them. First was Boy Scouts, then Little League, then soccer, and finally we settled back into the martial arts, which both boys had been studying since the age of 3.

A friend at work suggested that I sign the boys up for classes at the Naples Academy of Martial Arts, where her son trained. She said it was everything I was looking for: great people, a traditional philosophy, and a healthy atmosphere for the boys.

I wanted so badly for them to train, but couldn't afford the cost. My friend insisted that I call the sensei (teacher) at the dojo (martial arts school) and speak with her. I didn't know then how integral to my tribe that Sensei Hamilton and the dojo family would become to us. They would keep us together in the trial by fire that awaited us.

My First Day of Karate

Since I was a child, I had wanted to study martial arts. I used to watch my oldest brother practice karate and perform his katas. I was mesmerized, and remember trying to imitate him when no one was looking. But my parents could not afford karate lessons for me, and as an adult I never permitted myself that luxury either.

I called Sensei Deb Hamilton and explained our situation. She told me to come in with the boys and let them try it out, and then make the decision. It took only one class; the boys decided that they wanted to join. I was asked to join as well, but I decided that my children had to come first. Sensei knew our financial situation and she made it work for us. I think she sensed our love of training and wanted to make it happen for our family.

As the year went on, Sensei's daughter, Natasha, who also is a sensei at the dojo, was constantly after me to join. She told me that I needed to get off the sidelines and start training. I kept putting her off, because I knew that if I tried it out for a week, I would not want to stop. I just didn't think I could afford it.

That year, I was invited to the "train with your kid for Mother's Day" class. My sons asked me to join them in the class. They could see my love and admiration for that form of art, and they thought it would be awesome for us to do karate together. That was eight years ago, and since then I have not stopped training.

The Three of Us

This transformative activity changed my life in unimaginable ways. The boys and I developed a mutual respect and understanding through our training. When they were old enough, we began to train together in adult classes. It is so good to be able to train with them.

They were patient and supportive, and we trained together in and out of the dojo. It was amazing to see how naturally they picked up karate (taking judo from the age of 3 really helped). It was also amazing to see how they supported their less-than-coordinated mom who started training at the age of 43! Muscle memory is just not the same at that age. They were my constant support as I worked through belt after belt. Our dojo is very traditional, and belts are earned through hard work and study. The incredible thing is that all the people we trained with at the dojo were really nice.

Each one shared their knowledge with us and encouraged us to keep pushing forward. The dojo community gives back to our sensei through service projects in the community and volunteering at the dojo. The dojo has a philosophy that we should give back for the knowledge we receive. It was the perfect atmosphere for my children to grow up in.

Thanks to my friend, Elissa, who has trained with me now for the past eight years, we found an incredible community that became our happy place. Through our training, the boys and I have a bond that is incredibly strong. They are not mama's boys by any measure – but we know what each other is thinking, we share everything, and we are super close. We "get" each other, and I attribute that to a deep understanding that comes from training side-by-side for so long.

We realize that it's not just about getting the technique correct, but rather it is a mind, body, and spirit alignment that keeps one calm in the midst of turmoil. It is the realization that your mind can keep your body going, even after you think you cannot go on. Karate is the thing that held me together during my own health crisis.

Everything Changes

In July 2019, my back and shoulder were killing me. Because I train in martial arts, I thought that I had hurt myself in training. I am very used to working through pain and using meditation to stave it off, so I kept on meditating and training even though the pain was not dissipating.

I was concerned about the cost of treatment, so I did not go to the doctor until one day when I was moving some books at work. My shoulder seemed to give out. I was sent to six weeks of physical therapy to try to regain range of motion.

After six weeks, the shoulder was not improving, so I was sent for an MRI. That exam revealed that I had two tumors in my shoulder. One had fractured the scapula spine, and the other had eaten away most of my shoulder joint. All I could think was, *What the heck?*

I had no idea that I had been training with a fractured shoulder. I knew I was in pain, but tumors? Seriously? I remember calling my sister, Mary (who is an important part of my tribe) and joking with her that I would not be the first person who had not gone to the doctor for financial reasons and would end up having cancer.

Further tests showed that I had another tumor in my spine, which had eaten away two-thirds of a vertebra. I was diagnosed with multiple myeloma, a serious blood cancer which breaks down bone and does not allow it to be rebuilt. Suddenly, I went from a woman who was training in karate and Krav Maga six days a week – and close to earning a black belt – to someone who had 5 to 15 years left to live. That was **if** I was lucky and **if** the treatment worked. I found out that my bones were so fragile that I couldn't take any more intensive training – I would have to give up martial arts, and I was only 47 years old.

This Life Force

I have cancer, but what defines me is my faith in positive outcomes, and my love for my husband and my sons – not my cancer. I am blessed to have a strong husband beside me.

When I told Alberto the news, we decided that we would handle this as we did with Ander's cancer – as just another part of our everyday, normal life. We decided not to tell the boys until we knew exactly what lay ahead with the treatment protocol.

We finally had to share the news with the boys once I started radiation treatments, because the sessions were intense and sometimes made me sick. I was amazed at my sons' reaction. They accepted the information without question, and decided that they would work with me on my protocol, integrating a modified martial arts training schedule and supporting me where needed. Ander told me, "Well, Mom, now we are cancer buddies!"

Ander said, "Remember what you told me when I was sick, and I asked you if I could die? You told me it wasn't an option. The same goes for you now." Nicholas said, "Mom, it will be just like it was with Ander. You will go through your treatment and then go into remission. Everything will be fine." That is where I found my strength.

I realized that my children were watching my every move, and I could see their determination to help me succeed. I knew that I wanted to be an example for them. I needed them to see that even when you are at the top of your game in life, something quite serious can hit. But that does not mean you give up; rather, you find the strength inside to push forward and perform to the best of your ability.

Cancer treatment is very difficult, but I dug down into my soul and found my life force. I learned that all of the positive energy around you will carry you through, so that you can handle the crisis and move forward – always forward. Positivity does not mean you are happy all of the time. It means that you accept your present reality and understand that you have the power to change things. I focused on hope, and relentlessly refused to quit. I thought, *If I can show my children this and help them understand it, then I will have succeeded.*

The Choice to be Strong

Having incurable blood cancer forces a lot of reflection. I choose to have faith and be strong – because it is a choice. It is easy to give into the pain and the uncertainty. It is easy to imagine that every new pain is cancer causing more fractures. My karate training helps me to focus on the positive. I am determined to remember what is important to me, since it helps me know that I'm going to get through this. I'm moving forward. I say "yes" to life.

I have organized my response to my situation in the following manner: observe, tag and then move forward. I observe: *Wow, the chemo causes a lot of side effects that are painful;* I tag: *Well, that sucks;* and I move forward by employing a solution if possible, and if not, use meditation or martial arts to keep pushing on.

I choose to **respond** to every situation as it presents itself, instead of **reacting**. Reaction is without thought and is not helpful to me. This approach is essential for me, because there are so many triggers I could react to. The pain is constant. Whether it's the bone pain from where the tumors are, or the massive muscle cramps that wake me up every night because of the chemo, or the exhaustion that multiple myeloma brings, there is always something to react to.

By choosing to respond, it puts my situation back under my control. Responding allows me the luxury of deciding my own fate, as opposed to letting the cancer decide for me. When I put my gi (a loose-fitting martial arts uniform) on and go to the dojo with my boys to train, instead of giving into the pain and exhaustion, I am choosing a positive response and taking control of my experience. I focus on the love I have for my children, for my husband, for life. There is so much to love about life, and so much good in our world.

Our dojo family has supported us throughout my treatment. There was never a moment when I was allowed to give up. When my shoulder was fractured, the boys helped me put on a brace so I could continue training. Carlos Levia, one of the black belts, taught me to fight left-handed, since my right side was completely out of commission.

Carlos would say, "What, if someone attacked you and you had to defend your children, are you going to give up? Of course not! Figure it out!" Thanks to him, I did. That's why I say moving forward is a yes, or a yes. I love being a mom and I know that my children will be seriously affected by the outcome of my actions. So instead of focusing on the pain, I focus on the love I have for those whom I am fighting to stay alive for.

To me, love is the greatest gift we are given, and that love carries me through all the pain and uncertainty. I will be there for my family, because they have been there for me. Surviving is a yes, or a yes.

Pushing Forward

I will not let this cancer win.

So far, I have been through radiation, chemotherapy, and a stem cell transplant. I need to stay on maintenance chemo for the rest of my life to keep the cancer markers in my system at an acceptable number for survival. Chemo, in one word, "sucks." There are so many side effects, and the thought that there is no end to the treatment can be daunting. I just need to keep pushing forward, no matter the odds.

Every time that the thought of giving up surfaces, I challenge myself to push harder. I tell myself, *I am stronger than my cancer!* However, there are bad days when even meditation cannot contain the pain. I have gone so far as to mark down the days I get "out there," so that I can see a visual of how strong I am.

The philosophy of the dojo and the meaning of being a black belt is that you push yourself beyond your limits and dig down to find the strength to protect life. In this case, it's my life, and therefore the lives of those who depend on me. If I go down, my family goes down.

Alberto has already lost his father and one of his brothers to cancer. He doesn't need to also lose his wife to it because she decided to give up. The boys have been through so much, and have every reason to have issues and act out. Yet they have become fabulous human beings who care for others and make the world a much better place. How can I complain or even think about quitting? My family's strength inspires me to keep pushing forward.

Being An Outlier

Throughout my cancer journey, doctors have been perplexed by my condition. To begin with, this cancer usually attacks elderly people, and more often men. I am neither of those. When my scans came back at the beginning, my first doctor told me he could possibly extend my life from 5 to 15 years; but he also encouraged me to have hope, because new treatments were being developed.

I told him that I was not the sum of someone else's statistics, and I got a second opinion from a doctor who was an expert in multiple myeloma. She understood my need for martial arts training and just advised me to modify my routine accordingly.

I was told that I would have to stop doing karate due to the bone lesions. They might as well have told me to stop breathing. I explained to my doctors that my training was what kept me sane in an uncontrollable situation, and that there was absolutely no way I was stopping. I was in the process of training for a first-degree black belt, and I was not going to stop when I was so close to my goal.

I had a wonderful radiation oncologist, Dr. Bruce Nakfoor, who grew to understand my determination. He would tell me that I couldn't do this, and I couldn't do that. I finally stopped him and said, "Please, stop telling me what I can't do, and tell me what I can do." After that, he would work with me to let me know the specific movements that were allowed within the scope of my injuries due to cancer.

I was able to complete training and grading (evaluation) for first-degree black belt, which I passed. The doctors cannot explain how I was able to train so vigorously throughout treatment without getting sick. They applauded my tenacity, and said it has had a very positive effect on my treatment. I thank my children, husband, and dojo family for that! If I felt that I might be too tired, they would push me out the door to go train. The boys and my training partner, Elissa, trained alongside me seven days a week to keep me focused on my goal.

After the black belt grading, I had the stem cell transplant, which took me away from my family for three months. Again, I surprised the doctors. I was told that it was normal to become sick and be admitted to the hospital during the process, because the chemo completely knocks out the immune system. However, I never got sick.

I credit my sister Mary for helping me avoid sickness and hospitalization after the chemo. She stayed with me in Texas (where my doctors are) so my husband could stay home with the boys. She made sure that I took my meds and she disinfected everything to assure a sterile environment. Mary made sure I exercised – even the day after the procedure. I followed protocol to the letter, kept a journal, and of course kept training in martial arts. I started practicing tai chi, a gentler discipline, instead of karate.

Practicing Mindfulness

My oldest brother Joe, who is a master of meditation, made special recordings to help me with the side effects of the treatments. Thanks to the support, I was on my way back home to my family only three weeks after the transplant.

My doctors were amazed at my resilience, strength and determination. I joined research projects and provided samples of my blood and bone marrow, so researchers can find out how I am able to recuperate so quickly. I think it's due to the support from my tribe, the energy that's around me, and the energy that I take from the earth.

Everything empowers me to be who I am. I believe my resilience comes from the love I have around me and the love I feel towards my tribe, my family, my dojo family, our neighbors (who helped raise money to help our family), my school colleagues (who organized a silent auction as a fundraiser), and others who all came through for me.

An amazing energy of love and kindness helps me move ahead every day.

I have moments of doubt when the "new normal" of myeloma overwhelms me. However, when this happens, I meditate and visualize all the support I have received as a tangible energy that surrounds me. It moves me to a safe place where I can control the pain and the side effects of the chemo.

I will not let my people down by giving up. I will not let my boys or my husband down by giving up. I will not let myself down by giving up. I follow a Buddhist path, and I believe we are supposed to be conscientious with our actions while seeking enlightenment through kindness and compassion.

When Ander was so sick, I sat by his bed and thought with all my heart, *If anyone is listening to this, if cancer must come our way again, please give it to me. Do not let it touch my children ever again.* So, how can I be upset with my diagnosis? For me, this is many, many times better than having one of my children in this situation. I am truly at peace, and that gives me great strength.

The Dojo Became My Life

Training while having cancer treatments was an amazing time for me and the dojo, and my family there saved me. Three days each week, I would go to work, then go to my chemo treatment, and finally end the day with two hours of karate classes.

My boys were training right alongside me the entire time, which was an amazing feeling. My dojo family was essential to my success. It was amazing to feel how in control I was, even while going through chemo and knowing that my cancer was not curable. Martial arts grounded me. In the dojo, I wasn't the "lady with cancer," but rather another "karateka" who could surpass all expectations and push through.

I will be forever indebted to my sensei, my dojo family, and my husband and boys for the support they gave me throughout the journey to my black belt grading. The most memorable grading for me before black belt was my second stripe for brown belt. I had had a full day at work, and then went in for chemo treatment. After that, I showed up to the dojo to assist in a grading that was taking place that night.

Sensei Hamilton asked me, "Do you think you can do today what you did during training two days ago?" I said, "Of course, Sensei." She said, "Great! You are grading for your second stripe tonight!"

I still remember thinking, *Are you kidding? I just came off chemo treatment! I'm not sure how I am even standing up here, but OK! Here we go!*

That night, I pulled out everything I had. My boys were assisting in that grading, and I could feel their energy and the energy of my dojo family as I joined the grading. That was the most intense night of my life, and when I found out I had passed and had received my second stripe, I broke down and cried. Seeing the pride in my children's eyes was worth every drop of sweat spent that night.

A Black Belt in Life

As I look back on my journey at two of the most impactful elements of my life – karate and cancer – I see the synchronicities. Grading for black belt helped my recovery time with the chemo treatment, because I was in the best physical shape of my life (apart from the bone lesions on my shoulder, hips, skull, and spine). I was training seven days a week in preparation for the grading. That training helped my body to be strong enough to endure the chemo and prepare for the stem cell transplant.

The shodan (first-degree black belt) grading consists of three days of intensive training at boot camp from Friday to Sunday, and then a two-hour grading session. The idea is that you should be able to perform your martial arts even when you are mentally and physically exhausted.

For me, the grading was a metaphor for my chemo treatment. Chemo is poison, and you take that poison knowing it can cause horrible side effects, but you hope that it kills the cancer before it kills you. You need mental fortitude after your treatments, because you willingly submit yourself – day after day – to something that you know will make you feel incredibly ill.

How did I get through it? I truly believe that my training for shodan prepared me for my cancer treatment. Karate is life preservation, which means you can fight beyond your own strength to save those you love if they are threatened. When we fight or do katas, we visualize the battle that is happening. I envisioned my cancer. In every kata that I did during my grading, I was killing the cancer that threatened to take me away from my family. I was exhausted, but it didn't matter, because there was no way that I was letting the cancer win.

On the day of the grading, my boys, my senseis, and all of the black belts who had helped were there. I remember this incredible energy in our dojo. I was grading with Elissa, my training partner who has been by my side throughout my journey. It was truly incredible, because I could feel everyone pulling for me, and I drew off that energy to keep going until the end.

A shodan grading ends when you break eight boards in five seconds. The boards are set up in a circle, and you position them the way that you plan to break them. My youngest, Nicolas, was holding one of my boards. There was nothing but confirmation on his face that I would succeed in this last challenge before my grading ended, and I did succeed.

When I finished breaking all the boards, Nicolas hugged me and said, "You did it, Mom, you did it!" We both started crying. Ander came over, and then all three of us just held each other and cried. They were proud of their mom, who had overcome so much to finish such an intense grading. I was thankful to them for being the constant support and driving force that allowed me to succeed.

My husband, Alberto, joined us and we just held each other as a family. The love and support that had sustained me through my grading also sustained me through the stem cell transplant. I would not only survive, but I would thrive.

Leaving a Mark

Most people have no idea of what I go through daily, and I was never one to share. However, some people have asked me to share because it helps them find strength. If telling my story can help other people, then it is worth it.

The things that have helped me the most have been finding my tribe and pulling strength from their love and support. Every day is a learning experience, and every success is important – even if it's just getting through one minute at a time. Those minutes will add up to hours, which will add up to a day, and then many days, and that is how you keep moving in the right direction.

People have asked me why I have not crumbled under my diagnosis and how I am able to do all that I do. I just remember that I am not the sum of anyone's statistics, and if I can be at peace with my challenges and have hope in my heart, there is always a reason to keep moving forward.

If I were to give advice, I would say: find your purpose. Everything I do, every breath I take, everything I believe, every ounce of my being is for my two sons, Ander and Nicolas. Everything I do is an example for them. I am fighting so hard for them because I know how much they depend on me.

The SHEro Mindset

I have various tattoos; each symbolizes my life force. Two of them are linked to my children. One on my arm is an infinite loop with Ander and Nicolas written as part of the loop, and the words **"find strength"** written underneath. This tattoo is a reminder of why it is so important to pull myself up and keep moving forward.

People think you are supposed to be more enlightened after you have gone through cancer. What I gained was fortitude – fortitude to move forward and to love. This love can move mountains. When I look into my children's eyes every day, I know I'm doing the right thing.

My boys are 16 and 18 years old now, and the bond we have formed is unbreakable. I have enjoyed their journey in music. Nicolas plays oboe; Ander plays trumpet and recently joined a dance group at college. We have trained in karate together for the past eight years. Through that training, we deeply understand and respect each other. Supporting each other through difficult gradings in karate has built a mutual strength that has carried us through some of the most difficult times of our lives.

Yes, of course, I will survive. I choose not to be bitter, because I don't want to waste one second of my time being bitter when I'm with my boys. That's simply a waste of the time that we have with each other.

— DIDI ARPAIA

Inspiration to Have Faith

In life, we often focus on the verbs to do and to have, but *The SHEro Mindset* is about practicing the verb to BE. Use these suggestions to move through life with faith.

Be Hopeful
Moving through a dark tunnel, but knowing that there is light at the other end, is what hope looks like. What would your life look like if you had more hope? Hope can power our faith in ourselves, in others, and in the world.

Be Present
When we live in the present moment, we are able to have more faith. Honor your past, be present, and co-create your future. When you live in the now, you can experience the endless gifts of the present moment. You are the gift that you give to yourself in this moment.

Be Positive
All emotions are part of life, and they need to be felt and expressed. We are humans and we are here to live this life fully. But our attitude changes everything. Remaining calm and being positive allows us to have faith that we are supported by something larger than ourselves – maybe our higher self, maybe God.

Be Conscious

Be aware of your actions, thoughts and emotions. As we are aware of our responsibilities to ourselves and to others, we become one with the Divine. Then, Faith allows us to surrender and believe that everything has a purpose and all is in divine order.

Faith Meditation

Lift yourself like the lotus flower does
Through the mud and rise
Your struggles are the mud but you are the flower
Find the strength inside your core
Find your vital energy and rise
Like the beautiful lotus you are
Set your peace, and feel empowered
As you go through hard shifts
Connect to your higher power
Connect your core to the stars
Connect your core to the center of earth
Feel grounded
Breathe
There is a space in your heart
That can be only love
Go there
Stay there
Feel this quiet love
Faith will help you to be strong
Through your challenges
You will learn about your strengths
It will give you hope
That hope will keep you safe
It will give you courage
It will provide you an abundance of energy
To act with love and compassion towards your goals
Do not be distracted, accept what is presented

The SHEro Mindset

So you can experience the miracles
Stay connected to the source, it could be: connection to God, Buddha,
Or it could be your inner power
Don't be discouraged, do good in life, be a good person
Keep moving, keep going, keep searching, be open
Befriend the challenges, befriend your fears
The light is in you, above you and in front of you
Stay focused, never lose track, be persistent and
Let Faith take you through this journey called life!

Conclusion

What made this book possible? It was a combination of factors: my studies, my dedication to learning, my training with the power of Positive Psychology, and my meditation practice.

During these past four years, everything I did was related to the lessons of SPIRE – the Positive Psychology method that teaches how to learn and proactively balance the Spiritual, Physical, Intellectual, Relational and Emotional. For me, it is a simple and practical method that improves my wellness and quality of life. This method helped me immensely in my personal and professional life.

Positive Psychology and the Science of Happiness have allowed me to connect my story with my six SHEroes, through the virtues. We had so many things in common and I have been so honored to have them in my life as role models. I am still inspired by the stories of our SHEroes and how a positive mindset – combined with the essential virtues – can create a wonderful life.

During 2020, I was still grieving my mother's death. My husband and I feared we would lose our travel business due to the pandemic. We temporarily closed our nonprofit center for safety reasons. We also grieved the loss of many family members and friends. My son was thousands of miles away from us; I was worried about contracting COVID and not having any closure with him, since people were dying alone in hospitals. The fear was real.

I decided to stay positive, practice meditation, and immerse myself more deeply in the study of Positive Psychology. I was fortunate to be introduced to Positive Psychology by Dr. Dan Tamazulo at the Hudson Valley Psychodrama Institute in 2017. I became an alumna of Dr. Tal Ben-Shahar's Happiness Studies Academy in 2019.

I was certified as a Chief Happiness Officer by the World Happiness Summit (WOHASU) foundation and Florida International University, and had the pleasure of getting to know Karen Guggenheim, the founder of WOHASU.

In 2021, I finished my course as a coach in Positive Psychology from the Wholebeing Institute under Megan McDonough and Phoebe Atkinson. I was grateful to have these tools during the pandemic.

In 2022, I had an amazing transformation during the World Happiness Summit. I met the father of Positive Psychology, Dr. Martin Seligman. I had the opportunity to sit with him and share my heart and soul. I told him that I understand my purpose; my desire to connect to others, to leave my mark, and to empower others to find their purpose. I felt that we experienced a deep connection. Everything I have expressed

Conclusion

in this book is genuine and is offered with lots of love. I am grateful for my life, for my family, and for my students.

I am a SHEro because I chose to exercise solidarity (the feeling that brings us together as part of a greater whole) in my life. You too can be a SHEro! Everything is already inside of you – all of your super powers! What are you waiting for?

Reflections for a SHEro

Knowing ourselves well helps us to have a richer experience of life. *The SHEro Mindset* is meant to be an interactive experience. Take time to reflect on your life as you read this book.

For an even deeper experience, I have created an online companion to this book called *The SHEro Mindset* Workbook, which includes tools to develop and heal from a growth mindset. Visit my website, www.lulucarter.com, for more information on how to use this book and the workbook.

I encourage you to process all the inspirational stories you have read in this book by creating a journal. But before you start journaling, I encourage you to take the VIA Character Strengths Survey to find your own strengths and start utilizing them to experience a happier life:

https://www.viacharacter.org/survey/account/Register

Inspired to Write

As you write, the following questions will help you to reflect on your own story and will support you as you become your best self and develop your own SHEro mindset.

NOTE: *Have a notebook and something to write with. You can use colored pencils, crayons, water colors, and other fun art materials. You can create images as well as words.*

Your Caregivers & Friends
What influence did your parents, caregivers, friends and family members have on how you experience life?

Think about your own childhood heroes.

Who inspired you, cared for you, and helped you to grow?

The Environment
How did the environment of your childhood influence who you became?

Make a list of the places where you lived or traveled that impacted your development.

Who helped you to feel safe growing up?

Opportunities to Grow
Reflect on the doors (opportunities) that have closed in your life.

Make a list of them.

Now make a list of all the doors (opportunities) that opened in your life as a result of a door that was closed.

Reflect on these experiences.

Challenges

When did you use wisdom to learn from challenges?

Write down some examples of this.

Can you see challenges and disappointments as opportunities for growth?

Make a list of times you felt heartbroken.

Write what you learned from each incident.

Feelings

How do you relate to your feelings and emotions?

When do you accept them?

When do they interfere with your life?

When we feel lost or hopeless, we need to remind ourselves of positive things.

Take a moment to remember a time when you felt awake, aware or joyful.

Make a list of things that help you feel this way.

Your Support System

A SHEro also needs a support system to conquer adversity in life.

Take a moment to think about who is on your support team.

Write down their names. Take time to call them, thank them, and be part of others' needs for support.

If you don't have a support team yet, know that you can't do everything alone. It is never too late to build a group of people who share the same values as you do to help you go through life. Who would you like to have on your team?

Who do you support in life? Write down their names.

Role Models

We may believe that a hero, mentor or role model cannot have flaws or does not struggle. That is just a myth. We are all here to have the full range of human experiences and emotions.

Think about the setbacks in your life. What helped you to recover and reclaim your power?

Explore those experiences in your journal.

Forgiveness

Do you know how to forgive?

Do you have good role models who express forgiveness?

Are you able to forgive yourself?

Are you able to forgive the people in your life?

Survival

What have you done in your life in order to survive?

Make a list.

Do not be judgmental – instead, write with compassion.

Would you do anything differently now?

Creating

When we create, we are open to changes. We are in the flow of life! When we co-create with others, we are in harmony with the constantly-changing universe.

How often do you allow yourself to be creative, innovative, and take control of life?

Mothers and grandmothers are important in our lives.

How do you relate to your mother?

If you are a mother, what does it mean to you to be one?

Your SHEro mindset

How do you take care of your body, mind and soul with kindness?

How do you focus on your purpose?

How do you listen and follow your heart?

How do you practice compassion and forgiveness, for yourself and others?

Are you grateful for ALL of life's lessons?

Are you in service to others?

How do you love yourself unconditionally and embrace all of you? How are you authentic?

SPIRE

Do you practice the SPIRE (Spiritual, Physical, Intellectual, Relational, Emotional) model by addressing all parts of yourself?

What do you do, or what can you do, to feel more balanced?

Gratitude Practice

List the things you are grateful for, and what are the gifts in your life?

Life Lessons

What lessons have you learned so far in life?

What will your legacy be, once you leave this life?

I encourage you to journal about your legacy.

How often do you say YES to life?

Would you like to live a happier life?

What are your superpowers?

To learn more about how to practice SPIRE, and how to develop your SHEro mindset, please contact me at: lulu@lulucarter.com.

The 7 Angels

One for Each Day of the Week

The Angel of
FREEDOM

The Angel of Freedom is flying towards the horizon, and inspires us to follow the path of peace.

The Angel of
WISDOM

The Angel of Wisdom is standing on a rock, and inspires us to stay grounded, be reasonable, and make healthy choices.

The Angel of
JOY

The Angel of Joy is spreading its wings, and inspires us to feel joy and be grateful for life.

The Angel of
LOVE

The Angel of Love has its arms open, and inspires us to love ourselves first and spread that love to others.

The Angel of
COURAGE

The Angel of Courage is holding a sword, and inspires us to move forward in life and confront our fears.

The Angel of
CREATIVITY

The Angel of Creativity is standing on its power, and inspires us to connect with the Creator and find solutions.

The Angel of
FAITH

The Angel of Faith holds its hands close to its heart, and inspires us to stay calm, be patient, and have hope.

Acknowledgments

We are a collective sum of the many heroes who cross our paths. Living in gratitude, I want to acknowledge and thank those who made this book possible.

Thank you to my SHEroes and mentors who inspired me to find my true self and my voice: Regina Miranda, Angel Vianna, Shula Chernoff, Mary Bellofatto, Nancy Kirsner, Rebecca Walters, Karen Guggenheim, Megan McDonough and Phoebe Atkinson.

My family is my heart, and I am who I am because of them. To my aunt Gracinha, my cousins Paola and Denise, my uncle Douglas, my mother-in-law Irene, my husband Adam, and my son Mateus: thank you for your love and support.

My friends color my life and my sisterhood makes me stronger. Thank you Paula, Alexandra, Suely, Danica, Anna, Marjorie and my Gaia sisterhood.

I would also love to thank my editor Heather and my publisher April for their ideas, enthusiasm and encouragement during the process of creating this book.

Finally, I thank all of the women who have inspired me to be a better human.

About the Author

Born in São Paulo, Maria Luisa 'Lulu' Carter began her professional career in education, the arts, and community service in Rio de Janeiro, before moving first to Europe and then to the United States 26 years ago. With degrees from Brazil in speech therapy, art and psychodrama, and a Master's Degree in science and education from Southern Connecticut State University, Lulu views the world through an eclectic and multicultural prism.

Lulu has initiated projects that combine education, community service, and the arts throughout the world – including the Amazon, Haiti, Ghana and Bhutan. Lulu is the co-founder of Destination Partners, a travel management company that works with American universities, and also In-spire Us, a specialty travel company. Through these companies, Lulu has organized, created and developed educational programs abroad for Semester at Sea, New York University, the University of Virginia, and other American universities for the past 25 years.

In 2008, Lulu founded the nonprofit organization House of Gaia, in Naples, Florida, dedicated to bringing the world together through innovative programs and social inclusion. Lulu is a Chief Happiness Officer and is particularly interested in providing Positive Psychology services to individuals of all abilities.

Lulu's awards include: the Excellence in Diversity Award from Hodges University, in 2015; the Southwest Florida Face Award, in 2016; and the Lady Liberty Leader honor from Collier Freedom, in 2020.

For more about Lulu's work, please visit www.lulucarter.com.

www.ingramcontent.com/pod-product-compliance
Lightning Source LLC
Chambersburg PA
CBHW062033120526
44592CB00036B/1911